Praise for
Sarah Lynn and Bake To Be Fit

"If you're looking for a way to get your dessert fix, I'd definitely recommend Sarah's page! Her recipes look delicious, have fewer ingredients than it would take to make that pumpkin pie for Christmas (btw, she's got a recipe for that too), and I *promise*, you don't have to eat any kale to feel like a bonafide health goddess."

—Shannon Carney for SpoonUniversity.com

"As someone who has no food restrictions, I can personally attest to the fact that you do not have to be gluten-free to want to devour one of Sarah's desserts. One of the best brownies I have ever had, gluten-free or not, was one of Sarah's."

—Nako Kobayashi for friedmansprout.com

"Low-calorie dessert recipes that taste just as good as the real thing. *Almost* too good to be true."

—Krista Torres, for *Buzzfeed*

BAKE TO BE FIT

Secretly

Healthy Desserts

Easy Gluten-Free, Sugar-Free, Plant-Based, or Keto-Friendly Brownies, Cookies, and Cakes

SARAH LYNN

Skyhorse Publishing

Skyhorse Publishing books may be purchased in bulk at special discounts for sales promotion, corporate gifts, fund-raising, or educational purposes. Special editions can also be created to specifications. For details, contact the Special Sales Department, Skyhorse Publishing, 307 West 36th Street, 11th Floor, New York, NY 10018 or info@skyhorsepublishing.com.

Skyhorse® and Skyhorse Publishing® are registered trademarks of Skyhorse Publishing, Inc.®, a Delaware corporation.

Visit our website at www.skyhorsepublishing.com.

10 9 8 7 6 5 4 3 2 1

Library of Congress Cataloging-in-Publication Data is available on file.

Cover design by Laura Klynstra/Brian Peterson
Cover photo credit: Sarah Lynn

Print ISBN: 978-1-5107-4502-5

Printed in China

To my social media community,
for trusting and loving my recipes from the beginning.

Contents

Introduction

Welcome to my book of *Secretly Healthy Desserts*!

If you already own one of my e-books, welcome back, and thank you so much for your continued support. If you're new to my recipes, I am so excited for you to experience the joy that is healthy desserts!

I'm Sarah, owner and CEO of Bake to Be Fit. You may know me from my notoriously indulgent-looking dessert photos and videos on Instagram @sarahsfitfood. My passion is creating desserts that look and taste incredibly decadent but are secretly made with healthy ingredients.

My recipes have changed the lives of thousands, allowing people to incorporate delicious desserts into their diets on a regular basis without compromising their heath. I'm here to show you that whether you have dietary restrictions or allergies, or fitness/weight loss goals, or you choose to adhere to a special diet for any reason, you can still enjoy desserts (and they don't have to taste like cardboard).

Every recipe in this book was created, taste tested, and photographed by me. I hope you enjoy every single one, and I encourage you to share with friends and family. Even kids and picky eaters have been known to love these recipes, and no one will ever believe it when you tell them they are actually healthy.

For more delicious content, recipes, resources, and e-books, please feel free to check out my website and follow me on social media.

With Love & Healthy Desserts,
Sarah

The Healthy Baking Pantry

Here is a general guide to the ingredients I use in healthy baking. Keep in mind that this guide also includes substitution options, so not all of the ingredients mentioned here are necessary in order to make the recipes. I have also included an extensive shopping list to help you get started with building your healthy baking pantry.

Flours

Almond flour: Almond flour is created simply by pulsing whole almonds until the texture resembles flour. Blanched almond flour is made with almonds that have had their dark brown skins removed, so the resulting flour has a lighter, more uniform color. I recommend using fine-ground blanched almond flour for optimal appearance and texture of the finished product.

Coconut flour: Coconut flour is produced using dried coconut meat. The resulting flour has an extremely unique and absorbent texture. Because of this, only a small amount is needed, and it cannot be used as a 1-for-1 substitute for other flours. Coconut flour is very useful for creating recipes low in carbs and calories, as a small amount goes a long way.

Gluten-free oat flour: Oat flour is produced by pulsing oats until they turn into powder. Most stores sell premade oat flour, but it is also easy to make your own by pulsing dry oatmeal in your blender or food processor. If you need to make your recipes 100 percent gluten-free, always make sure to purchase certified gluten-free oats or oat flour.

Starches: Starches are very helpful in gluten-free baking, as the texture they contribute helps resemble the texture that gluten adds to baked goods. My preferred types of starches are tapioca and arrowroot starch, however, cornstarch or potato starch can also be substituted.

Gluten-free all-purpose flour: Gluten-free all-purpose flour is a blend of several different gluten-free flours that creates a similar texture to wheat-based all-purpose flour. Different brands vary in what flours they use in the blend, but most brands should work in recipes that call for gluten-free all-purpose flour. If you do not need to eat a gluten-free diet, you may be able to substitute wheat-based all-purpose flour in my recipes, but I have not tried this myself.

Cocoa Powder

Dutch process vs. regular: Dutch-process cocoa has been treated with an alkalizing agent to give it a neutral pH, while regular cocoa has an acidic pH. Dutch-process cocoa has a darker color and smoother flavor than regular cocoa and is often used in brownies and other dark chocolate desserts. I recommend using Dutch-process cocoa when called for in the recipes to achieve the most authentic flavor. The pH does affect the overall recipe, so if regular cocoa powder is substituted, keep in mind that the texture, flavor, and color of the finished product may be slightly altered.

Sweeteners

In general, granulated sweeteners can be used interchangeably with each other, and liquid sweeteners can be used interchangeably with each other. Of course, any time a substitution is made, it may affect the outcome of the recipe, but sweeteners are generally very easy to substitute if you have a preferred sweetener. Some sweeteners vary in sweetness—for example, you may need more unrefined cane sugar to achieve the same sweetness as ¼ cup erythritol—and sometimes just a few drops of pure stevia can sweeten an entire recipe, so keep these variations in mind when making substitutions.

Unrefined natural sweeteners: Unrefined sweeteners provide more nutrients than refined sugar. They have not gone through a refining process, which removes the naturally occurring nutrients and minerals. They do contain some dietary sugars, so a sugar-free natural sweetener option may be preferred for those who are not able to consume any dietary sugars.

Examples of unrefined natural sweeteners:
- Coconut palm sugar
- Unrefined organic cane sugar (also called evaporated cane juice or turbinado sugar)
- Pure maple syrup
- Honey

Sugar-free natural sweeteners: Sugar-free natural sweeteners are ideal for those who are not able to consume dietary sugars, those who follow a ketogenic diet, or anyone wanting to reduce total sugar or carb intake. They can also be combined with any unrefined natural sweetener to reduce total sugar content in a recipe, a strategy I use in many of my recipes.

Examples of sugar-free natural sweeteners:
- Erythritol (granulated and powdered)
- Stevia
- Monk fruit
- Xylitol

Note: Stevia comes in many different forms, including baking blends and pure extract. Measurement needed will vary depending on the form of stevia being used.

Want a tip for reducing sugar while almost eliminating any aftertaste of sugar-free sweeteners? Use half regular sweetener and half sugar-free sweetener. For example, if a recipe calls for 1 cup powdered erythritol (a sugar-free sweetener), use ½ cup regular powdered sugar and ½ cup powdered erythritol. This still drastically reduces sugar and calorie content, while almost completely eliminating any aftertaste of the erythritol.

Protein Powder

Some of the recipes call for flavored whey protein powder as an ingredient, adding extra dietary protein, texture, flavor, and sweetness. In the recipes that call for whey protein powder, the protein powder functions as an important component of the recipe, and omitting it will affect the texture and flavor of the finished product (unless specified).

The recipes have been tested using stevia-sweetened whey protein isolate, which is approximately 28 grams in weight per "scoop," and each scoop contains approximately 100 calories and 25 grams of protein. Other types of protein powders will also work in the recipes. All dairy-derived protein powders, with the exception of casein protein, will work similarly to whey protein isolate. Pure casein protein tends to absorb more liquid than whey protein, so slightly more liquid may need to be added when using pure casein protein if the mixture seems dry.

Dairy-derived protein powders:
- Whey protein isolate
- Whey protein concentrate
- Whey + casein blend
- Casein protein

If you are unable to consume dairy-based protein for any reason, dairy-free protein powders may be substituted. Using dairy-free protein, such as a pea/brown rice protein blend, may result in a slightly different texture than using whey

protein, although still delicious in its own way. For example, cakes and banana breads may have a slightly denser, less fluffy texture.

Dairy-free protein powders:
- Pea/brown rice protein blends (plant based)
- Egg-white protein powder (vegetarian)
- Collagen protein powder (bovine or marine derived)

Note: Collagen protein does not change texture of baked goods as significantly as other protein powders, so it can be added to recipes as an extra add-in but should not be used as a substitute for whey protein powder when called for.

Egg Replacement

Many of the recipes are already egg-free, so I would recommend first trying those if you are intolerant/allergic to eggs, choose to follow a plant-based diet, or are unable to consume eggs for any other reason.

If you'd like to experiment with substituting eggs in the recipes that call for them, you may try using a "flax egg" or another method of egg replacement, however, results are not guaranteed.

Your Healthy Dessert Shopping List

Flours & Dry Ingredients
- Fine-ground blanched almond flour
- Coconut flour
- Gluten-free oat flour
- Gluten-free all-purpose flour
- White or brown rice flour
- Tapioca or arrowroot starch
- Gluten-free quick oats
- Vanilla whey protein powder
- Chocolate whey protein powder

Sweeteners
- Coconut palm sugar
- Unrefined cane sugar
- Granulated erythritol
- Powdered erythritol
- Stevia baking blend
- Pure maple syrup
- Honey

Fat Sources
- Grass-fed unsalted butter
- Dairy-free butter
- Virgin coconut oil
- Refined coconut oil
- Avocado oil
- Peanut butter
- Cashew butter
- Almond butter

Leavening Agents
- Baking soda
- Baking powder
- Eggs

Other
- Dutch-process cocoa powder
- Regular cocoa powder
- Golden ground flaxseed meal
- Fine-grain sea salt or Himalayan pink salt
- Canned white beans
- Canned unsweetened pumpkin puree
- Unsweetened applesauce
- Unsweetened almond milk, or milk of choice

Add-ins/Flavorings/Decorations
- Chocolate chips
- Sugar-free chocolate chips
- White chocolate chips
- Macadamia nuts
- Walnuts
- Shredded coconut
- Pure vanilla extract
- Peppermint extract
- Sprinkles (all-natural, if desired)
- Food coloring (all-natural, if desired)

Allergen/Dietary Restriction Guide

Allergen substitution notes are included below each recipe. If there is not a suggested substitution recommended for your allergen on any particular recipe, it means that I do not recommend substituting for that ingredient. When baking with an allergy, always make sure to check the label on each ingredient used to make sure they do not contain traces of your allergen.

Wheat/Gluten

All of the recipes in this book are both wheat- and gluten-free, making them suitable for anyone with gluten intolerance/sensitivity, gluten allergy, wheat allergy, or celiac disease, or those who are avoiding dietary wheat or gluten for any reason.

Soy

None of the recipes in this book contain soy-based ingredients. However, always check the ingredients on chocolate chips, as many brands contain sneaky "soy lecithin," which is used as an emulsifier.

Dairy

Many of the recipes call for dairy-based ingredients, but luckily almost all the recipes can be easily adjusted to suit a dairy-free diet. Check the substitution notes on each individual recipe for recommendations for adjusting the recipe with dairy-free alternatives. Make sure your chocolate chips are dairy-free.

Lactose

For those with lactose intolerance, I recommend mostly following the dairy-free substitution notes on each recipe. However, some dairy-derived protein powders have been processed to remove the lactose, so they may be tolerated by those with lactose intolerance (but not those with a milk protein allergy). Look for whey protein isolate that indicates lactose-free on the label.

Tree Nuts

Aside from the recipes that call for almond flour or nut butters, most of the recipes are tree nut–free. Follow the nut-free substitution notes on each recipe for guidance on how to make substitutions for any nut ingredients.

Peanuts

Many of the recipes are peanut free. Peanut butter can always be replaced with sunflower-seed butter (in the case of peanut allergies that also include tree nuts) or any other nut butter.

Eggs

Many of the recipes are egg-free as written. In the recipes that do call for eggs, feel free to experiment with "flax eggs" or other forms of egg replacement, however, results are not guaranteed.

Nutritional information:

Each recipe includes calculations of total calories, grams of fat, net carbs, protein, fiber, and sugar per serving. These calculations have been made based on standard nutritional listings for each ingredient but may vary slightly by brand.

Net carbs are a calculation of total carbohydrates, minus fiber and sugar alcohols. Net carbs are thought to be the carbs that have the most effect on blood sugar, so many people choose to count net carbs instead of total carbs. To calculate total carbs, add grams of fiber + grams of net carbs + grams of sugar alcohols (if applicable).

The nutritional information for cakes, brownies, and frostings/toppings are listed separately to allow you to mix and match recipes with different frostings and toppings, unless otherwise specified. Likewise, the allergen icons (see next page) refer only to the ingredients listed on that page, and do not cover suggested frostings or toppings that have ingredients listed on separate pages.

Allergen Icons

Icons are placed on each recipe page to indicate the lack of presence of common allergens. It is the baker's responsibility to check the label of each ingredient used to ensure there are no hidden allergens present or risk of cross-contamination during the manufacturing process of the ingredient.

G Gluten-free: This icon indicates that there are no gluten-containing ingredients in the recipe. This icon applies to every recipe, as all the recipes in this book are gluten-free.

G Grain-free: This icon indicates that there are no gluten-free grains present in the recipe, such as rice, corn, or oats. Examples of grain-free flours used are almond flour, coconut flour, tapioca starch, and arrowroot starch.

N Nut-free: This icon indicates that there are no nuts present in the ingredients of the recipe. This nut-free icon considers peanuts a nut, even though peanuts are technically a legume, so look for the nut-free icon if you have either a peanut or tree-nut allergy. The nut-free icon does not consider coconut a nut, as coconut is technically a fruit, and most individuals with nut allergies are able to consume coconut. Make adjustments accordingly if you are not able to consume coconut ingredients.

D Dairy-free: This icon indicates that there are no dairy-derived ingredients included in the recipe.

S Sugar-free: This icon indicates that there are no sugar-containing sweeteners added to the recipe.

E Egg-free: This icon indicates that there are no eggs used in the recipe.

K Keto: This icon indicates that the recipe adheres to the guidelines for the ketogenic diet. These recipes do not contain any sugar containing natural sweeteners or other carb sources, and have net carb content of less than 7 grams per serving.

P Plant-based: This icon indicates that the recipe does not include any ingredients from animal sources, such as dairy or eggs.

Triple-Layer Chocolate Cake, page 2

Cakes, Cupcakes & Quick Breads

Triple-Layer Chocolate Cake

Serves: 12

147 Calories / 10 g Fat / 9 g Net Carbs / 4 g Protein / 3 g Fiber / 6 g Sugar

INGREDIENTS:

1 cup blanched almond flour (112 g)
¼ cup coconut flour (28 g)
¼ cup tapioca or arrowroot starch (36 g)
¼ cup Dutch-process cocoa powder (20 g)
5 tablespoons coconut sugar (60 g)
5 tablespoons erythritol (60 g)
2 teaspoons baking powder
½ teaspoon salt
½ cup unsweetened applesauce (120 g)
3 tablespoons avocado oil (42 ml)
2 eggs
1 teaspoon vanilla extract
Keto Cream Cheese Frosting (page 190)
Chocolate Protein Frosting (page 164)

 G Gluten-free
D Dairy-free

INSTRUCTIONS:

1. Preheat oven to 350°F. Spray three 6-inch round cake pans with nonstick oil spray.
2. Combine all dry ingredients in a bowl.
3. In a separate large bowl, whisk together all wet ingredients.
4. Pour dry into wet, and stir gently just until combined.
5. Distribute batter between the three pans and spread out evenly with a spatula or back of a spoon.
6. Bake for 14 to 16 minutes, being careful not to overbake.
7. Allow to cool before removing from pans.
8. Layer Keto Cream Cheese Frosting in between layers, then frost with Chocolate Protein Frosting. Slice and enjoy! Store in the refrigerator.

Nut-free option: Use all-purpose gluten-free flour instead of almond flour

Keto option: Use sugar-free sweetener, replace tapioca with almond flour, and replace applesauce with extra oil or butter.

Pumpkin Spice Latte Cupcakes

Serves 12

192 calories / 14.5 g Fat / 7.5 g Net Carbs / 5 g Protein / 2.5 g Fiber / 6.5 g Sugar

INGREDIENTS:

1½ cups blanched almond flour (168 g)
¼ cup coconut flour (28 g)
3 teaspoons baking powder
½ teaspoon salt
⅓ cup coconut palm sugar (64 g)
⅓ cup erythritol (64 g)
½ teaspoon cinnamon
2 teaspoons pumpkin pie spice
½ teaspoon ginger
6 tablespoons butter, melted (84 g)
½ cup pumpkin puree (120 g)
3 eggs
1 teaspoon vanilla
Espresso Frosting (page 165)
Vanilla Whipped Cream (page 186)
Ground espresso, for topping

G Gluten-free
G Grain-free

INSTRUCTIONS:

1. Preheat oven to 350°F. Line a muffin tin with cupcake liners or grease pan.*
2. Combine all dry ingredients in a large bowl.
3. Add butter and stir, then add pumpkin, eggs, and vanilla.
4. Stir just until combined—do not overmix.
5. Distribute batter between the cupcake liners or greased wells.
6. Bake for 20 to 22 minutes, and allow to cool.
7. Prepare Espresso Frosting and Vanilla Whipped Cream.
8. Using a knife, cut approximately 1-inch-wide by 1-inch-deep holes in the top of each cupcake. Fill each hole with a heaping tablespoon of whipped cream.
9. Add the frosting to an icing bag, or a plastic sandwich bag with a corner cut off, and pipe frosting onto each cupcake.
10. Sprinkle each cupcake with ground espresso if desired, and enjoy!
11. Store covered in the refrigerator.

*If you do not use cupcake liners, you may need to decrease baking time by a few minutes.

Dairy-free option: Use dairy-free butter.

Nut-free option: Use sunflower-seed flour instead of almond flour.

Keto option: Use sugar-free sweetener instead of coconut sugar.

Tip! Make your own pumpkin pie spice blend by combining 3 tablespoons ground cinnamon, 2 teaspoons ground ginger, 1½ teaspoons ground nutmeg, 1 teaspoon ground allspice, and 1 teaspoon ground gloves. Mix well and measure out as needed when pumpkin pie spice is called for.

Keto "Brookie" Marble Swirl Pound Cake

Serves 12

153 calories / 13 g Fat / 2.5 g Net Carbs / 5 g Protein / 3.5 g Fiber / 0.5 g Sugar

INGREDIENTS:

1 cup blanched almond flour (112 g)
3 tablespoons coconut flour (21 g)
⅓ cup erythritol (64 g)
1½ teaspoons baking powder
¼ teaspoon salt
½ cup ricotta (124 g)
¼ cup butter, melted (56 g)
2 eggs
1 teaspoon vanilla extract
2 tablespoons cocoa powder (10 g)
5 tablespoons sugar-free chocolate chips (56 g)

G Gluten-free
K Keto
S Sugar-free
G Grain-free

Dairy-free option: Use dairy-free butter.

Nut-free option: Use sunflower-seed flour instead of almond flour.

INSTRUCTIONS:

1. Preheat oven to 350°F. Line two mini loaf pans* with parchment paper.
2. Combine all dry ingredients (except cocoa powder and chocolate chips) in a large bowl, then add ricotta, melted butter, eggs, and vanilla.
3. Mix just until combined. Be careful not to overmix.
4. Spoon about ⅓ of the batter into a separate bowl, and stir in cocoa powder.
5. Fold 2 tablespoons of the chocolate chips into the batter with cocoa powder, and 3 tablespoons into the remaining batter.
6. Spoon some of the vanilla batter into the bottoms of the pans, and spread evenly. Then spread a layer of chocolate batter into the pans, reserving a few tablespoons. Spread the remaining vanilla batter over the chocolate batter, then spoon the remaining chocolate batter on top. Note: this sequence of layering can be done however you wish; this is just an explanation of how I achieved the appearance pictured.
7. Top with extra chocolate chips, if desired.
8. Bake for 35 to 37 minutes.
9. Allow to cool, slice, and enjoy!

*You may also bake this recipe in one standard-sized 8 x 4–inch loaf pan and increase baking time by about 10 minutes.

Coffee Cake

Serves: 16

162 Calories 11 g / Fat / 9.5 g Net Carbs / 3.5 g Protein / 2 g Fiber / 7.5 g Sugar

INGREDIENTS:

Cake:
1¾ cups blanched almond flour (196 g)
¼ cup tapioca starch (36 g)
2 tablespoons ground flax (14 g)
3 tablespoons coconut sugar (36 g)
3 tablespoons erythritol (36 g)
1½ teaspoons baking powder
½ teaspoon salt
¼ cup unsweetened applesauce (60 g)
2 tablespoons avocado oil (30 ml)
2 eggs
½ teaspoon vanilla extract

Cinnamon Streusel:
3 tablespoons butter, melted (42 g)
6 tablespoons coconut sugar (72 g)
1 tablespoon coconut flour (7 g)
1 tablespoon cinnamon (8 g)
Keto Icing Drizzle (page 183)

 Gluten-free
Ⓖ Grain-free

INSTRUCTIONS:

1. Preheat oven to 350°F. Grease an 8x8-inch baking dish, or line with parchment paper.
2. Combine dry cake ingredients in a large bowl, then add wet ingredients and stir just until combined.
3. Put cake batter aside while you prepare the cinnamon streusel. Combine all streusel ingredients in a small bowl and stir until combined.
4. Spread half the cake batter into the bottom of the pan. Drizzle half of the cinnamon streusel mixture over the batter, then cover with the remaining cake batter.
5. Drizzle the remaining half of the streusel on top of the cake batter. Then take a knife and gently run it though the cake from side to side to swirl the streusel through the cake.
6. Bake for 25 to 30 minutes.
7. Allow to cool, then drizzle with Keto Icing Drizzle, if desired. Enjoy!

Dairy-free option: Use dairy-free butter.

Nut-free option: Use all-purpose gluten-free flour instead of almond flour.

Keto option: Use sugar-free sweetener, replace tapioca with almond flour, and replace applesauce with extra oil or butter.

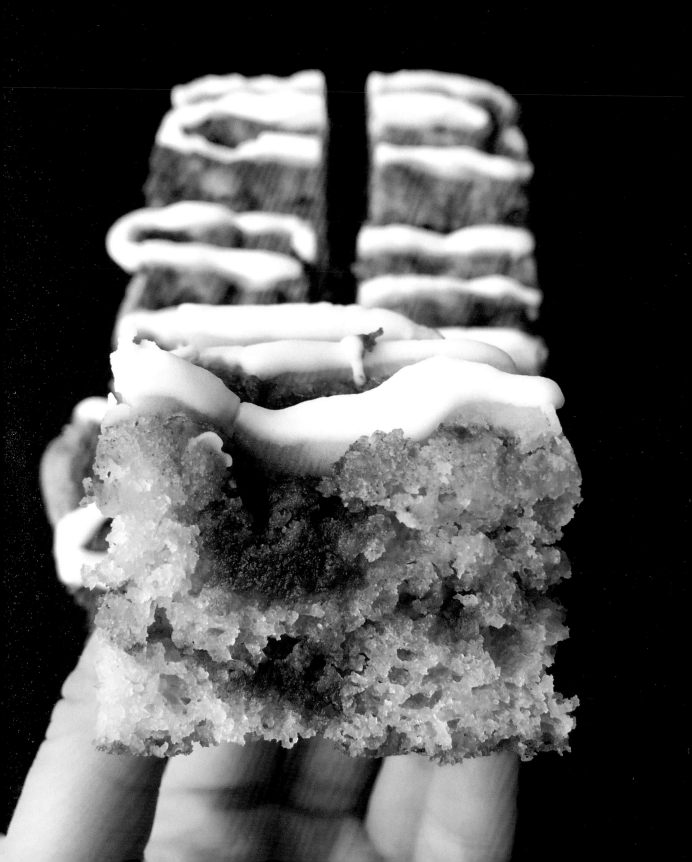

Keto Vanilla Sheet Cake

Serves 12

105 calories / 9.5 g Fat / 1 g Net Carbs / 3 g Protein / 1.5 g Fiber / 0 g Sugar

INGREDIENTS:

¾ cup blanched almond flour (84 g)
2 tablespoons ground flaxseed (13 g)
2 tablespoons coconut flour (14 g)
½ cup erythritol (96 g)
1½ teaspoons baking powder
¼ teaspoon salt
5 tablespoons butter, melted (70 g)
2 eggs, beaten
2 teaspoons vanilla extract
Keto Chocolate Fudge Frosting (page 185)

(G) Gluten-free
(K) Keto
(S) Sugar-free
(G) Grain-free

INSTRUCTIONS:

1. Preheat oven to 350°F. Line an 8x8-inch pan with parchment paper.
2. Combine all dry ingredients in a large bowl, then add butter, eggs, and vanilla.
3. Mix just until combined—do not overmix.
4. Pour batter into pan and spread out evenly with the back of a spoon.
5. Bake for 25 to 27 minutes, until a toothpick inserted into the center comes out clean.
6. Allow to cool, then frost with Keto Chocolate Fudge Frosting, or frosting of choice. Slice and enjoy!

Tip! To make a double-layer cake, double the recipe and bake in two 8x8-inch pans.

Dairy-free option: Use dairy-free butter.

Nut-free option: Use sunflower-seed flour instead of almond flour.

Keto Chocolate Chip Pound Cake

Serves 12

145 calories / 12.5 g Fat / 2 g Net Carbs / 5 g Protein / 3 g Fiber / 0.5 g Sugar

INGREDIENTS:

1 cup blanched almond flour (112 g)
3 tablespoons coconut flour (21 g)
⅓ cup erythritol (64 g)
1½ teaspoons baking powder
¼ teaspoon salt
½ cup ricotta cheese (124 g)
¼ cup butter, melted (56 g)
2 eggs, beaten
1 teaspoon vanilla extract
¼ cup sugar-free chocolate chips (56 g)
Keto Icing Drizzle (page 183)

(G) Gluten-free
(K) Keto
(S) Sugar-free
(G) Grain-free

INSTRUCTIONS:

1. Preheat oven to 350°F. Line two mini loaf pans* with parchment paper.
2. Combine all dry ingredients (except chocolate chips) in a large bowl, then add ricotta, melted butter, beaten eggs, and vanilla.
3. Mix just until combined, then fold in chocolate chips. Be careful not to overmix.
4. Pour batter into pans and spread out evenly with the back of a spoon.
5. Bake for 35 to 37 minutes.
6. Allow to cool, then drizzle with icing if desired. Slice and enjoy!

*You may also bake this recipe in one standard-sized 8x4–inch loaf pan and increase baking time by about 10 minutes.

Dairy-free option: Use dairy-free butter.

Nut-free option: Use sunflower-seed flour instead of almond flour.

Keto Carrot Cake

Serves 12

110 calories / 9 g Fat / 2 g Net Carbs / 3.5 g Protein / 2 g Fiber / 1 g Sugar

INGREDIENTS:

¾ cup blanched almond flour (84 g)
¼ cup coconut flour (28 g)
1½ teaspoons baking powder
¼ teaspoon salt
⅓ cup erythritol (64 g)
2 tablespoons unsweetened shredded coconut (10 g)
1 teaspoon cinnamon
½ teaspoon ginger
1 cup shredded carrots (128 g)
¼ cup butter, melted (56 g)
2 eggs
⅓ cup ricotta cheese (82 g)
1 teaspoon vanilla extract
Keto Cream Cheese Frosting (page 190)

Ⓖ Gluten-free
Ⓚ Keto
Ⓢ Sugar-free
Ⓖ Grain-free

INSTRUCTIONS:

1. Preheat oven to 350°F. Line an 8x8-inch pan with parchment paper.
2. Combine all dry ingredients in a large bowl.
3. Whisk wet ingredients (including carrots) together in a separate bowl. Pour dry into wet.
4. Stir just until combined—do not overmix.
5. Pour batter into pan and spread out evenly with the back of a spoon.
6. Bake for 30 minutes, or until cake is cooked through in the center.
7. Allow to cool, then frost with Keto Cream Cheese Frosting. Slice and enjoy!

Dairy-free option: Use dairy-free butter.

Nut-free option: Use sunflower-seed flour instead of almond flour.

Keto Pumpkin Spice Cupcakes

Serves 12

170 calories / 14.5 g Fat / 1.5 g Net Carbs / 5 g Protein / 2 g Fiber / 1 g sugar

INGREDIENTS:

1½ cups blanched almond flour (168 g)
3 tablespoons ground flax (20 g)
3 teaspoons baking powder
½ teaspoon salt
¾ cup erythritol (144 g)
1½ teaspoons pumpkin spice
1½ teaspoons cinnamon
¾ teaspoon ginger
6 tablespoons pumpkin puree (90 g)
6 tablespoons butter, melted (84 g)
3 eggs
1 teaspoon vanilla extract
Keto Cream Cheese Frosting (page 190)
Vanilla Whipped Cream (page 186)

G Gluten-free
K Keto
S Sugar-free
G Grain-free

INSTRUCTIONS:

1. Preheat oven to 350°F. Line a muffin tin with cupcake liners or grease pan.*
2. Combine all dry ingredients in a large bowl.
3. Add butter and stir, then add pumpkin and eggs.
4. Stir just until combined—do not overmix.
5. Distribute batter between the cupcake liners or greased wells.
6. Bake for 20 to 22 minutes.
7. Allow to cool, then frost with Keto Cream Cheese Frosting and Vanilla Whipped Cream, if desired. Enjoy!

*If you do not use cupcake liners, you may need to decrease baking time by a few minutes.

Dairy-free option: Use dairy-free butter.

Nut-free option: Use sunflower-seed flour instead of almond flour.

Donut Muffins

Serves 12

176 calories / 10 g Fat / 19 g Net Carbs / 2.5 g Protein / 1.5 g Fiber / 10 g Sugar

INGREDIENTS:

Muffins:
1½ cups all-purpose gluten-free flour (222 g)
⅓ cup unrefined cane sugar (64 g)
2 teaspoons baking powder
¼ teaspoon salt
¼ cup ricotta cheese (57 g)
½ cup unsweetened almond milk (120 ml)
5 tablespoons unsalted butter, melted (70 g)
1 egg

Coating:
5 tablespoons butter, melted (70 g)
½ cup unrefined cane sugar (96 g)
2 teaspoons cinnamon

Ⓖ Gluten-free
Ⓝ Nut-free

INSTRUCTIONS:

1. Preheat oven to 375°F. Line a muffin tin with liners.
2. Combine flour, sugar, baking powder, and salt in a large bowl. Add wet muffin ingredients and stir just until a thick batter forms.
3. Fill muffin cups about halfway full.
4. Bake for 18 to 20 minutes. Allow to cool.
5. While muffins are cooling, melt the remaining 5 tablespoons of butter in a small bowl.
6. In a separate bowl, combine sugar and cinnamon.
7. Remove liners from each muffin.
8. One muffin at a time, lightly coat in melted butter, then coat in cinnamon sugar. Repeat for remaining muffins.
9. Donut muffins may be served immediately. Warm in the microwave as needed for an extra soft and doughy texture. Enjoy!

Dairy-free option: Use ½ cup dairy-free butter instead of the butter and ricotta cheese in the muffins, and use dairy-free butter for coating.

Sugar-free option: Use sugar-free sweetener.

Note: Extra cinnamon/sugar mixture and butter is needed in order to make sure all muffins get coated. You will not use all of the sugar coating or all of the butter. Therefore, only ¼ cup of the coating sugar and 4 tablespoons of the butter have been counted in nutritional information. Extra cinnamon sugar can be saved and used as a topping or coating for other recipes.

Keto Tiramisu

Serves 12

240 calories / 22 g Fat / 3.5 g Net Carbs / 5.5 g Protein / 0.8 g Fiber / 1.5 g Sugar

INGREDIENTS:

Sponge cake "ladyfingers":
¾ cup blanched almond flour (84 g)
¼ cup powdered erythritol (48 g)*
¼ cup baking stevia
½ teaspoon baking powder
¼ teaspoon salt
½ cup ricotta cheese (114 g)
2 eggs
½ teaspoon vanilla

Custard:
4 egg yolks
2 tablespoons whole milk (30 ml)
½ cup powdered erythritol (96 g)*
1½ cups mascarpone (240 g)

Whipped Cream:
1 cups heavy whipping cream (240 ml)
2 tablespoons powdered erythritol (24 g)*
½ teaspoon vanilla

Additional:
¼ cup brewed espresso (60 ml)
1–2 tablespoons spiced rum (15 ml, optional)
Unsweetened cocoa powder, for dusting

*You may substitute unrefined cane sugar or powdered sugar for the erythritol if you do not need this recipe to be sugar-free or keto.

Ⓖ Gluten-free
Ⓚ Keto
Ⓢ Sugar-free
Ⓖ Grain-free

INSTRUCTIONS:

1. Preheat oven to 350°F. Line an 8x8-inch baking dish with parchment paper.
2. Make sponge cake: Combine dry ingredients in a large bowl. Add ricotta, eggs, and vanilla, and stir just until combined.
3. Spread batter evenly into parchment-lined pan.
4. Bake for about 30 minutes or until firm in the center.
5. While the sponge cake is baking, prepare custard: In a double boiler, combine egg yolks, milk, and sweetener. Cook, whisking constantly, for about 8 to 10 minutes until the mixture turns a creamy lemon color and slightly thickens.
6. Remove the custard from heat and allow to cool for about 5 minutes before adding the mascarpone. Stir until completely smooth. Place custard in the refrigerator to cool.
7. Prepare whipped cream: Add heavy cream to a large bowl. Using an electric mixer with whisk attachment, beat on medium speed until stiff peaks form.
8. Fold about one quarter of the whipped cream into the cooled custard.
9. To assemble tiramisu: Slice sponge cake into 16 long, thin slices. Place 8 of the slices cut-side down on the bottom of an 8x8-inch glass baking dish.
10. Mix together espresso and optional rum in a small bowl. Brush the sponge cake slices with the espresso mixture.

11. Layer in half of the custard mixture, followed by half of the remaining whipped cream. Dust with cocoa powder.

12. Layer in the remaining sponge cake slices, then brush with espresso.

13. Repeat step 11 with the remaining custard and whipped cream, finishing with a dusting of cocoa powder.

14. Allow to set in the refrigerator for at least 4 hours before slicing and serving.

15. Slice and enjoy! Store in the refrigerator.

Lower-fat option: Use skim or lower-fat alternatives for the ricotta, milk, and mascarpone.

Nut-free option: Use sunflower-seed flour instead of almond flour.

Red Velvet Cake for Two

Serves 2

113 calories / 2.5 g Fat / 10 g Net Carbs / 9 g Protein / 5 g Fiber / 3.5 g Sugar

INGREDIENTS:
2 tablespoons coconut flour (14 g)
2 tablespoons oat flour (15 g)
½ scoop vanilla or chocolate whey protein powder (14 g)
2 tablespoons erythritol or baking stevia
1 tablespoon cocoa powder (5 g)
1 teaspoon ground flaxseed
¼ teaspoon baking soda
⅛ teaspoon salt
1 teaspoon maple syrup
1 teaspoon oil
3 tablespoons unsweetened applesauce (45 g)
¼ cup unsweetened almond milk (60 ml)
5 drops red food coloring (optional)
Cream Cheese Frosting I (page 191)

G Gluten-free
E Egg-free

INSTRUCTIONS:
1. Preheat oven to 350°F.
2. Combine all dry ingredients in a mixing bowl.
3. Add wet ingredients and stir just until combined.
4. Divide the batter between two greased 5-inch ramekins.
5. Bake for 15 to 18 minutes, checking after 15 minutes.
6. Allow to cool before frosting and serving.
7. Make cream cheese frosting, and frost each cake separately. For a double-layer cake, layer the two frosted cakes on top of each other, then cut in half. Share with a friend and enjoy!

Plant-Based/Dairy-free option: Use dairy-free and/or plant-based protein powder.

Nut-free option: Use nut-free milk instead of almond milk.

Sugar-free option: Use sugar-free syrup instead of maple syrup.

75-Calorie Classic Chocolate Cake

Serves 9

75 calories / 0.8 g Fat / 6 g Net Carbs / 9.5 g Protein / 3 g Fiber / 3 g Sugar

INGREDIENTS:

1 can pumpkin puree (15 oz./425 g)
1 cup nonfat plain Greek yogurt (227 g)
3 tablespoons coconut flour (21 g)
⅓ cup Dutch-process cocoa powder (27 g)
½ cup erythritol or baking stevia
2 scoops chocolate whey protein powder (56 g)
1 tablespoon arrowroot starch (7 g)
½ teaspoon baking soda
¼ teaspoon salt
½ teaspoon instant coffee powder (optional, for richer chocolate flavor)
Vanilla Cream Frosting and Filling (page 174)
Chocolate Ganache (page 150)

Ⓖ Gluten-free
Ⓝ Nut-free
Ⓢ Sugar-free
Ⓔ Egg-free
Ⓖ Grain-free

INSTRUCTIONS:

1. Preheat oven to 350°F. Grease an 8x8-inch square glass pan with nonstick spray, or line with parchment paper..

2. Either by hand or in a blender or food processor, combine pumpkin and yogurt.

3. In a separate bowl, combine all dry ingredients and stir. Pour the dry ingredients into the pumpkin/yogurt mixture, and blend until well combined.

4. Scoop batter into greased pan.

5. Bake for 40 to 45 minutes or until firm in the center. Allow to cool before slicing and serving. I recommend refrigerating this cake until completely cool before frosting. Store covered in the refrigerator.

6. Slice and frost with Vanilla Cream Frosting and Chocolate Ganache, or frosting of choice.

Fudge Brownie Cake

Serves 9

138 calories / 6.5 g Fat / 13 g Net Carbs / 7 g Protein / 4 g Fiber / 8 g Sugar

INGREDIENTS:

¼ cup coconut flour (28 g)
¼ cup tapioca or arrowroot starch (30 g)
½ cup Dutch-process cocoa powder (40 g)
1½ scoops chocolate whey protein powder (42 g)
⅓ cup erythritol or baking stevia
1 teaspoon ground flaxseed meal
½ teaspoon baking soda
¼ teaspoon salt
½ cup unsweetened applesauce (113 g)
¼ cup nonfat plain Greek yogurt (113 g)
2 tablespoons pure maple syrup (30 ml)
¼ cup unsweetened almond milk (60 ml)
2 tablespoons coconut oil, melted (28 g)
¼ cup chocolate chips (60 g)
Cookie Dough Frosting (page 166)
Chocolate Ganache (page 150)

G Gluten-free
E Egg-free
G Grain-free

INSTRUCTIONS:

1. Preheat oven to 325°F. Grease an 8x8-inch square glass pan with nonstick spray, or line with parchment paper.
2. In a large bowl, combine all dry ingredients except chocolate chips. Add applesauce, yogurt, maple syrup, and almond milk. Stir just until combined.
3. Add coconut oil and stir until combined. Fold in chocolate chips, if desired.
4. Scoop batter into the greased pan.
5. Bake for 17 to 20 minutes, being careful not to overbake.
6. Allow to cool before frosting with Cookie Dough Frosting and Chocolate Ganache, if desired. Slice and enjoy!

Plant-based/Dairy-free option: Use dairy-free and/or plant-based protein powder, and replace Greek yogurt with applesauce.

Nut-free option: Use nut-free milk instead of almond milk.

Sugar-free option: Use sugar-free syrup instead of maple syrup, and use sugar-free chocolate chips.

Mini Double-Layer Brownie Cake

Serves 4

80 calories / 2.5 g Fat / 7 g Net Carbs / 6 g Protein / 3 g Fiber / 4 g Sugar

INGREDIENTS:

2 tablespoons coconut flour (14 g)
2 tablespoons gluten-free oat flour (15 g)
¾ scoop chocolate whey protein powder (21 g)
2 teaspoons coconut sugar
3 tablespoons erythritol or baking stevia
2 tablespoons cocoa powder (10 g)
1 teaspoon ground flax
¼ teaspoon baking soda
⅛ teaspoon salt
1 teaspoon avocado oil
¼ cup unsweetened applesauce (60 g)
3 tablespoons unsweetened almond milk (45 ml)
½ teaspoon vanilla extract
Cookie Dough Frosting (page 166)
Chocolate Brownie Frosting (page 167)

 Gluten-free
Egg-free

INSTRUCTIONS:

1. Preheat oven to 350°F. Spray two 5-inch ramekins with nonstick oil spray.
2. Combine all dry ingredients in a mixing bowl. Add wet ingredients and stir just until combined.
3. Divide batter between the two ramekins.
4. Bake for 15 to 20 minutes, or until slightly firm in the center. Be careful not to overbake.
5. Allow to cool, and layer with cookie dough and chocolate frosting if desired.

Plant-based/Dairy-free option: Use dairy-free and/or plant-based protein powder.

Nut-free option: Use nut-free milk instead of almond milk.

Sugar-free option: Use sugar-free sweetener instead of coconut sugar.

1-Minute Chocolate Peanut Butter Cake

Serves 1

140 calories / 1.5 g Fat / 12.5 g Net Carbs / 14.5 g Protein / 4.5 g Fiber / 3.5 g Sugar

INGREDIENTS:

1 tablespoon coconut flour (7 g)
2 teaspoons tapioca starch (6 g)
½ scoop chocolate whey protein powder (14 g)
1 tablespoon cocoa powder (5 g)
1 tablespoon erythritol or baking stevia
⅛ teaspoon baking soda
3 tablespoons unsweetened applesauce (45 g)
2 tablespoons unsweetened almond milk (30 ml)
Peanut Butter Frosting (page 181)
Chocolate chips, for topping (optional)

Ⓖ Gluten-free
Ⓢ Sugar-free
Ⓔ Egg-free
Ⓖ Grain-free

INSTRUCTIONS:

1. Combine all dry cake ingredients in a small mixing bowl.
2. Add applesauce and almond milk. Stir just until combined.
3. Spray a 5-inch microwave-safe bowl or ramekin with nonstick spray and scoop in your cake batter.
4. Microwave in 30 second intervals until done. Total cooking time should be around 1 minute. Be careful not to overcook.
5. Allow to cool while you prepare the Peanut Butter Frosting.
6. Invert cake onto a plate, and top with frosting.
7. Cut in half and stack the halves on top of each other.
8. Drizzle with peanut butter and top with chocolate chips, if desired. Enjoy!

Plant-based/Dairy-free option: Use dairy-free and/or plant-based protein powder.

Nut-free option: Use nut-free milk instead of almond milk, and use a different frosting instead of Peanut Butter Frosting.

Mini Double-Layer Carrot Cake

Serves 4

79 calories / 3 g Fat / 6 g Net Carbs / 4.5 g Protein / 3 g Fiber / 3 g Sugar

INGREDIENTS:

2 tablespoons coconut flour (14 g)
2 tablespoons gluten-free oat flour (15 g)
½ scoop vanilla whey protein powder (14 g)
2 tablespoons erythritol or baking stevia
1 teaspoon coconut palm sugar
¼ teaspoon baking soda
⅛ teaspoon salt
1 teaspoon ground flaxseed
1 teaspoon avocado oil
⅓ cup shredded carrots (48 g)
1 tablespoon shredded coconut (4 g)
1 tablespoon chopped walnuts (7 g) (optional)
¼ teaspoon cinnamon
½ teaspoon vanilla extract
¼ cup unsweetened applesauce or crushed
   pineapple (60 g)
3 tablespoons unsweetened almond milk (45 ml)
Cream Cheese Frosting II (page 192)

Ⓖ Gluten-free
Ⓔ Egg-free

INSTRUCTIONS:

1. Preheat oven to 350°F.
2. Combine the first 8 cake ingredients in a mixing bowl.
3. Add oil, shredded carrots, coconut, nuts (if desired), cinnamon, and vanilla. Then add applesauce and almond milk.
4. Stir just until combined, being careful not to overmix.
5. Spray two 5-inch ramekins with nonstick spray and divide cake batter evenly between the two ramekins.
6. Bake for 16 to 18 minutes. Be careful not to overbake. Allow to cool completely while you prepare the Cream Cheese Frosting.
7. Layer the two cakes with frosting, then frost the sides. Garnish with extra shredded carrots, chopped nuts, and coconut flakes, if desired. Slice into four pieces and enjoy! Store in the refrigerator.

Note: You may also choose to bake these into 4 muffins or cupcakes.

Plant-based/Dairy-free option: Use dairy-free and/or plant-based protein powder.

Nut-free option: Use nut-free milk instead of almond milk, and omit chopped walnuts.

Sugar-free option: Use sugar-free sweetener instead of coconut sugar.

Cinnamon Streusel Banana Bread

Serves: 18

72 calories / 2.5 g Fat / 7 g Net Carbs / 4 g Protein / 2 g Fiber / 3.7 g Sugar

INGREDIENTS:

Banana bread:
½ cup coconut flour (56 g)
½ cup gluten-free oat flour (56 g)
2 tablespoons ground flaxseed meal (14 g)
2 scoops vanilla whey protein powder (56 g)
2 tablespoons coconut palm sugar (24 g)
⅓ cup baking stevia
2 teaspoons cinnamon
½ teaspoon baking powder
½ teaspoon baking soda
¼ teaspoon salt
2 ripe bananas, mashed (250 g)
½ cup unsweetened almond milk (120 ml)
1 teaspoon vanilla extract
1 tablespoon coconut oil or butter, melted (14 g)

Streusel:
2 teaspoons butter or coconut oil, softened (10 g)
1 tablespoon coconut flour (7 g)
2 teaspoons coconut palm sugar (8 g)
2 teaspoons erythritol or baking stevia
½ teaspoon cinnamon

G Gluten-free
E Egg-free

INSTRUCTIONS:

1. Preheat oven to 350°F.
2. Add all dry banana bread ingredients to a large bowl and stir well.
3. Add banana, almond milk, vanilla extract, and butter or oil. Stir just until combined—do not overmix.
4. Line two mini* loaf pans with parchment paper or spray with nonstick spray. Divide batter evenly between the two pans.
5. Combine all streusel ingredients in a small bowl and mix until a crumbly texture is achieved.
6. Divide streusel on top of the two loaves.
7. Bake for 30 to 35 minutes.
8. Allow to cool, and slice each loaf into 9 pieces. Enjoy!

*You may also bake this recipe in one standard-sized 8x4–inch loaf pan, but you may need to increase the baking time.

Plant-based/Dairy-free option: Use dairy-free and/or plant-based protein powder.

Nut-free option: Use nut-free milk instead of almond milk.

Sugar-free option: Use sugar-free sweetener instead of coconut sugar.

Chocolate Chip Banana Bread

Serves: 18

73 calories / 2.5 g Fat / 8 g Net Carbs / 4 g Protein / 2 g Fiber / 4 g Sugar

INGREDIENTS:

½ cup coconut flour (56 g)
½ cup gluten-free oat flour (56 g)
2 tablespoons ground flaxseed meal (14 g)
2 scoops vanilla whey protein powder (56 g)
2 tablespoons coconut palm sugar (24 g)
⅓ cup baking stevia
2 teaspoons cinnamon
½ teaspoon baking powder
½ teaspoon baking soda
¼ teaspoon salt
2 ripe bananas, mashed (250 g)
½ cup unsweetened almond milk (120 ml)
1 teaspoon vanilla extract
1 tablespoon butter or coconut oil, melted (14 g)
2 tablespoons mini chocolate chips (30 g)

 Gluten-free
 Egg-free

INSTRUCTIONS:

1. Preheat oven to 350°F.
2. Add all dry banana bread ingredients except chocolate chips to a large bowl and stir well.
3. Add banana, almond milk, vanilla extract, and butter or oil. Stir just until combined—do not overmix.
4. Fold in chocolate chips.
5. Line two mini loaf pans with parchment paper or spray with nonstick spray.
6. Divide batter evenly between the two pans.
7. Add extra chocolate chips onto the tops, if desired.
8. Bake for 30 to 35 minutes.
9. Allow to cool, and slice each loaf into 9 slices. Enjoy!

*You may also bake this recipe in one standard-sized 8x4-inch loaf pan, but you may need to increase the baking time.

Plant-based/Dairy-free option: Use dairy-free and/or plant-based protein powder.

Nut-free option: Use nut-free milk instead of almond milk.

Sugar-free option: Use sugar-free sweetener instead of coconut sugar, and use sugar-free chocolate chips.

Cookie Dough–Filled Funfetti Cupcakes

Serves 12

110 calories / 4.5 g Fat / 8 g Net Carbs / 6.5 g Protein / 3.7 g Fiber / 3.8 g Sugar

INGREDIENTS:

¾ cup coconut flour (84 g)

½ cup gluten-free oat flour (56 g)

2 scoops vanilla- or birthday-cake-flavored protein powder (56 g)

½ teaspoon baking powder

½ teaspoon baking soda

½ teaspoon salt

2 tablespoons ground flaxseed (12 g)

⅓ cup erythritol or baking stevia

¾ cup unsweetened applesauce (180 g)

2 tablespoons coconut oil, melted (28 g)

2 tablespoons pure maple syrup (30 ml)

1¼ cup unsweetened almond milk (300 ml)

¼ cup sprinkles (optional)

Edible Cookie Dough Filling II (page 178)

Keto Cream Cheese Frosting (page 190) or Vanilla Cream Frosting (page 174)

G Gluten-free

E Egg-free

INSTRUCTIONS:

1. Preheat oven to 350°F. Grease a muffin tin or line with cupcake liners.
2. Combine all dry ingredients in a large bowl.
3. Add wet ingredients and beat just until combined.
4. Fold in sprinkles if using.
5. Bake for 17 to 20 minutes.
6. Allow to cool, and scoop out a hole in each cupcake for the cookie dough.
7. Fill with cookie dough frosting or filling, then frost with vanilla or cream cheese frosting of choice.

Plant-based/Dairy-free option: Use dairy-free and/or plant-based protein powder.

Nut-free option: Use nut-free milk instead of almond milk.

Sugar-free option: Use sugar-free syrup instead of maple syrup.

5-Ingredient Flourless Chocolate Fudge Cake with Chocolate Ganache

Serves 9

252 calories / 10 g Fat / 22 g Net Carbs / 18 g Protein / 4 g Fiber / 7 g Sugar

INGREDIENTS:

2 large sweet potatoes, baked, skin
   removed (~700 g)
2 cups nonfat plain Greek yogurt (450 g)
⅓ cup virgin coconut oil (80 g)
4 scoops chocolate whey protein powder (112 g)
1 cup Dutch-process cocoa powder (80 g)
Stevia or maple syrup to taste, only if needed

(G) Gluten-free
(N) Nut-free
(S) Sugar-free
(E) Egg-free
(G) Grain-free

Plant-based/Dairy-free option: Use dairy-free and/or plant-based protein powder, and replace Greek yogurt with either extra sweet potato, dairy-free yogurt, or a combination of the two.

INSTRUCTIONS:

1. Preheat oven to 350°F. Grease an 8x8-inch glass pan, or line with parchment paper.
2. In a food processor or high-speed blender, combine sweet potato, Greek yogurt, and coconut oil, and blend until smooth.
3. Add protein powder and cocoa powder and blend until very smooth and silky.
4. Taste test the batter and add stevia or maple syrup to taste. Reserve about one-quarter to one-third of the batter in a covered container and place in the refrigerator to thicken (this will be the chocolate ganache). Spread remaining batter evenly into pan.
5. Bake for 15 to 20 minutes, or until slightly firm in the center.
6. Allow to set in the refrigerator for several hours or preferably overnight, then frost with chocolate ganache. Slice and enjoy! Store in the refrigerator.

Note: This cake is dense and rich. Use more coconut oil for an even richer, fudgier texture, or use less to lighten it up. Do not use fewer than 3 tablespoons, as some coconut oil is needed to achieve a firm texture.

Variation: Use a whey + casein protein powder blend, or 100% casein protein powder, for an extra firm, dense texture.

Flourless Chocolate Peanut Butter Cookie Dough Cake

Serves 6

287 calories / 14 g Fat / 21 g Net Carbs / 18 g Protein / 7 g Fiber / 11 g Sugar

INGREDIENTS:

Cake:
1 large sweet potato, baked, skin removed (~350 g)
½ cup nonfat plain Greek yogurt (113 g)
2½ tablespoons coconut oil (35 g)
2 scoops chocolate whey protein powder (56 g)
⅓ cup cocoa powder (27 g)
Stevia or maple syrup to taste, only if needed

Peanut Butter Chocolate Chip Cookie Dough:
¼ cup coconut flour (28 g)
½ scoop vanilla whey protein powder (14 g)
2 tablespoons coconut palm sugar (24 g)
⅛ teaspoon salt
¼ cup peanut butter (64 g)
¼ cup almond milk (60 ml)
2 tablespoons chocolate chips (30 g)

Note: Nutritional info includes everything listed.

Ⓖ Gluten-free
Ⓔ Egg-free
Ⓖ Grain-free

INSTRUCTIONS:

1. Preheat oven to 350°F. Grease an 8x4-inch glass pan, or line with parchment paper.
2. In a food processor or blender, combine sweet potato, Greek yogurt, and coconut oil, and blend until smooth.
3. Add protein powder and cocoa powder and blend until very smooth.
4. Taste test the batter and add stevia or maple syrup to taste. Reserve one-third of the batter in a covered container and place in the refrigerator to thicken (this will be the chocolate ganache).
5. Spread remaining batter evenly into pan. Bake for 15 to 20 minutes, or until slightly firm in the center. Allow to set in the refrigerator for several hours or preferably overnight.
6. Once cake and ganache have set, make the cookie dough: Combine all dry ingredients except chocolate chips in a small bowl. Add peanut butter and mix until distributed. Slowly add almond milk until desired consistency is reached. Fold in chocolate chips.
7. Spread cookie dough evenly over cake, then top with chocolate ganache. Slice in 6 pieces, and enjoy!

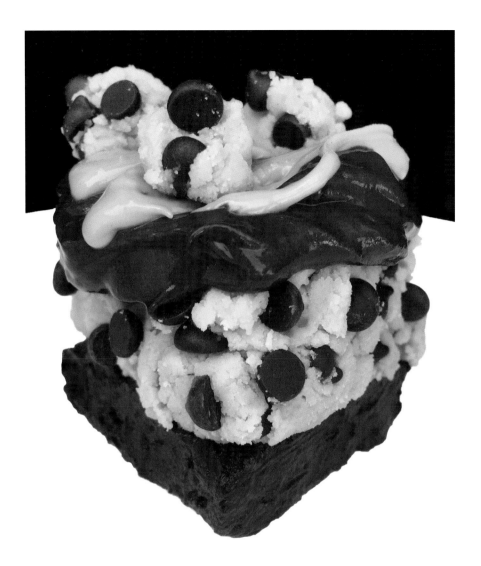

Plant based/Dairy-free option: Use dairy-free and/or plant-based protein powder, and replace Greek yogurt with extra sweet potato, dairy-free yogurt, or a combination of the two.

Nut-free option: Use nut-free milk instead of almond milk and use sunflower-seed butter instead of peanut butter.

Sugar-free option: Use sugar-free sweetener instead of coconut sugar.

Fudge Brownie Cookie Dough Cake

Serves 4

202 calories / 8.5 g Fat / 18.5 g Net Carbs / 12 g Protein / 5 g Fiber / 9 g Sugar

INGREDIENTS:

2 servings Fudge Brownie Cake (page 27)
1 recipe classic chocolate chip cookie dough, unbaked
1 recipe chocolate fudge frosting (see below, or other chocolate frosting recipes included in the frostings section can be substituted)
1 tablespoon almond butter or peanut butter (16 g)

Classic chocolate chip cookie dough:

1½ tablespoons coconut flour (10 g)
2 tablespoons tapioca or arrowroot starch (14 g)
⅓ scoop vanilla protein powder (9 g)
2 teaspoons coconut palm sugar
⅛ teaspoon salt
1 teaspoon coconut oil, melted
2 tablespoons applesauce (30 g)
⅛ teaspoon vanilla extract
1 tablespoon mini chocolate chips (15 g)

Chocolate Fudge Frosting:

2 tablespoons Dutch-process cocoa powder (10 g)
2 tablespoons powdered peanut butter (13 g)
½ scoop chocolate whey protein powder (14 g)
3 tablespoons powdered erythritol (36 g)
¼–⅓ cup unsweetened almond milk (60–80 ml)

Ⓖ Gluten-free
Ⓔ Egg-free
Ⓖ Grain-free

INSTRUCTIONS:

1. Prepare Fudge Brownie Cake in advance and allow to cool.
2. Combine all dry cookie dough ingredients in a small bowl. Add coconut oil and distribute throughout dry ingredients. Add remaining ingredients and stir until a dough forms. Set aside.
3. Prepare frosting by adding all dry ingredients to a small bowl, then slowly adding almond milk until you achieve the desired texture.
4. Take your two squares of brownie cake and top each square with cookie dough, distributing the dough evenly between the two squares.
5. Next, spread frosting on top of the cookie dough. Slice each square in half diagonally, to create four triangles. Drizzle each triangle with nut butter, if desired. Serve, and enjoy!

Note: Nutritional information for this recipe includes everything listed.

Plant-based/Dairy-free option: Use dairy-free and/or plant-based protein powder.

Nut-free option: Use nut-free milk or water instead of almond milk, and use a nut-free drizzle option instead of almond butter. Use a different topping instead of the chocolate fudge frosting, as it contains peanut butter powder.

Sugar-free option: Use sugar-free sweetener instead of coconut sugar.

The Best Protein Cheesecake

Serves 9

113 calories / 6 g Fat / 4.7 g Net Carbs / 10 g Protein / 0 g Fiber / 4.5 g Sugar

INGREDIENTS:

1 cup reduced-fat cream cheese (227 g)
1½ cups nonfat plain Greek yogurt (340 g)
1½ scoops vanilla whey protein powder (42 g)
1 egg
1 egg white
½ cup powdered erythritol or baking stevia
1 tablespoon pure maple syrup (15 ml)
1 teaspoon vanilla extract

Ⓖ Gluten-free
Ⓝ Nut-free
Ⓖ Grain-free

INSTRUCTIONS:

1. Preheat oven to 325°F. Allow cream cheese to come to room temperature.
2. Mix all ingredients either by hand, in a blender, or with an electric mixer.
3. Pour into an 8x8-inch pan sprayed with nonstick oil spray, or line with parchment paper.
4. Bake for 15 minutes, reduce the temperature to 200°F, and bake for 40 more minutes.
5. Allow to cool, then chill in the refrigerator for at least 4 to 6 hours or overnight before slicing and serving.
6. Top with toppings of choice, and enjoy!

Tip! To make using a cookie dough crust as pictured, make a batch of Plant-based Cookie Dough from page 135 and press cookie dough into the bottom of the parchment-lined pan, then pour cheesecake batter over the cookie dough layer. Bake according to regular instructions above.

Keto option: Use full-fat cream cheese, full-fat Greek yogurt or sour cream instead of non-fat yogurt, and use sugar-free syrup instead of maple syrup, or omit the syrup.

Sugar-free option: Use sugar-free syrup instead of maple syrup, or omit the syrup.

Keto Pumpkin Cheesecake with Sugar Cookie Crust

Serves 12

146 calories / 13 g Fat / 2 g Net Carbs / 3.5 g Protein / 1 g Fiber / 1 g Sugar

INGREDIENTS:

Sugar Cookie Crust:
¾ cup almond flour (84 g)
2 tablespoons coconut flour (14 g)
2 tablespoons erythritol (24 g)
⅛ teaspoon salt
3 tablespoons butter, softened (42 g)

Cheesecake:
1 cup cream cheese, softened (224 g)
6 tablespoons pumpkin puree (90 g)
1 egg
¾ cup powdered erythritol (144 g)
½ teaspoon pumpkin spice
½ teaspoon cinnamon
Vanilla Whipped Cream (page 186)
Cinnamon, for dusting (optional)

Ⓖ Gluten-free
Ⓚ Keto
Ⓢ Sugar-free
Ⓖ Grain-free

INSTRUCTIONS:

1. Preheat oven to 325°F. Line an 8x8-inch pan with parchment paper.
2. Start with crust: Combine dry ingredients in a bowl, then add softened butter and mix until a dough forms. Press dough into bottom of pan.
3. Bake crust for 7 minutes, then remove from oven.
4. Now assemble cheesecake ingredients: Add cream cheese, pumpkin, and egg to a bowl, and beat until smooth. Stir in powdered erythritol and spices, then beat again until fully combined.
5. Pour cheesecake mixture over crust and spread so that the cheesecake is evenly covering the crust.
6. Return to oven and bake for 35 minutes.
7. Allow to cool, then refrigerate for at least 4 to 6 hours or overnight before slicing and serving.
8. Top with Vanilla Whipped Cream and a sprinkle of cinnamon immediately before serving, if desired. Enjoy!

Dairy-free option: Use dairy-free butter and cream cheese.

Nut-free option: Use sunflower-seed flour instead of almond flour.

Crustless Pumpkin Pie

Serves 8

114 calories / 0.5 g Fat / 14.7 g Net Carbs / 11 g Protein / 2 g Fiber / 8.5 g Sugar

INGREDIENTS:

1 (15-oz.) can pumpkin puree (425 g)
¾ cup unsweetened almond milk (180 ml)
3 scoops vanilla whey protein powder (84 g)
¼ cup all-purpose gluten-free flour (37 g)
2 tablespoons tapioca starch (15 g)
⅓ cup coconut sugar (64 g)
1½ teaspoons pumpkin pie spice
½ teaspoon salt
Vanilla Whipped Cream (page 186)

 Gluten-free
Egg-free

INSTRUCTIONS:

1. Preheat oven to 375°F.
2. Add all ingredients to a large bowl and beat with electric mixer until smooth. You may also blend in a blender or food processor.
3. Pour into a greased or parchment paper–lined 9-inch pie pan, or into a premade crust, if desired.
4. Bake for 35 to 40 minutes.
5. Allow to cool completely and then refrigerate for at least 6 hours or overnight before serving.
6. Slice, and top with whipped cream, if desired. Enjoy!

Plant-based/Dairy-free option: Use dairy-free and/or plant-based protein powder.

Nut-free option: Use nut-free milk instead of almond milk.

Sugar-free option: Use sugar-free sweetener instead of coconut sugar.

Brownies

The Ultimate Chocolate Fudge Brownies

Serves 16

78 calories / 2.5 g Fat / 8 g Net Carbs / 5 g Protein / 2 g Fiber / 3.5 g Sugar

INGREDIENTS:

1 can white beans (~240 g after draining and rinsing*)
¼ cup unsweetened applesauce (60 g)
2 tablespoons butter or coconut oil (28 g)
¼ cup unsweetened almond milk (60 ml)
1 teaspoon vanilla extract
2 scoops chocolate protein powder (56 g)
¼ cup gluten-free quick oats (23 g)
⅓ cup Dutch-process cocoa powder (30 g)
3 tablespoons coconut sugar (36 g)
⅓ cup erythritol or baking stevia
3 tablespoons chocolate chips, melted (45 g)
½ teaspoon baking powder
¼ teaspoon baking soda
¼ teaspoon salt

*I used butter beans, but cannellini beans or navy beans will also work. These beans are extremely neutral in flavor, and there is no flavor from the beans. Black beans can be used, but I find they can have a stronger flavor.

Ⓖ Gluten-free
Ⓝ Nut-free
Ⓔ Egg-free

INSTRUCTIONS:

1. Preheat oven to 325°F. Line an 8x8-inch glass baking dish with parchment paper.
2. In a food processor or high-speed blender (such as a Vitamix), blend drained and rinsed beans, applesauce, butter or oil, almond milk, and vanilla.
3. Add protein powder, quick oats, cocoa powder, coconut sugar, and stevia. Blend until combined.
4. Add chocolate, baking powder, baking soda, and salt, and blend just until combined.
5. Spread into parchment-lined pan.
6. Bake for 15 to 18 minutes.
7. Allow to cool, and frost with chocolate buttercream frosting.
8. Slice into 16 pieces, and enjoy! Store in the refrigerator.

Tips: I recommend underbaking these for best results; they may seem underdone when they first come out of the oven, but after setting and cooling, they will be perfectly firm and fudgy. Refrigerate for a few hours before enjoying for ultimate fudgy-ness.

Plant-based/Dairy-free option: Use plant-based and/or dairy-free protein powder.

Sugar-free option: Use sugar-free sweetener instead of coconut sugar and use sugar-free chocolate chips.

Healthy Breakfast Brownies

Serves 1

268 calories / 8 g Fat / 27 g Net Carbs / 17 g Protein / 7.5 g Fiber / 9.5 g Sugar

INGREDIENTS:

⅓ cup gluten-free quick oats (32 g)
½ cup water (120 ml)
½ scoop chocolate whey protein powder (14 g)
2 tablespoons unsweetened almond milk (30 ml)
1 teaspoon coconut oil
2 tablespoons Dutch-process cocoa powder (10 g)
4 stevia packets, or about 2–3 tablespoons baking stevia
2 teaspoons pure maple syrup
½ teaspoon ground flaxseed
1 tablespoon chocolate chips (15 g; optional, not included in nutritional information)
¼ teaspoon baking powder
⅛ teaspoon salt
¼ teaspoon vanilla extract
Vanilla Whipped Cream (see page 186)
Greek yogurt, for topping

G Gluten-free
E Egg-free

INSTRUCTIONS:

1. Preheat oven to 325°F.
2. Line a 7x5-inch glass baking pan with parchment paper.
3. Combine oats and water in a microwave-safe bowl. Microwave for 1 minute and 30 seconds.
4. Add protein powder, almond milk, oil, and cocoa powder and stir until combined.
5. Then stir in stevia, maple syrup, flax, and chocolate chips, if desired. Stir until chocolate chips are completely melted.
6. Add baking powder, salt, and vanilla, and stir just until combined.
7. Spread into parchment-lined pan.
8. Bake for 11 to 13 minutes.
9. Allow to cool and top with whipped cream or Greek yogurt, if desired. Slice into 6 pieces, and enjoy! I enjoy these even more if they have been refrigerated for a few hours after cooling. Great to make ahead the night before!

Note: Recipe makes one 5 x 7-inch pan of brownies. Nutritional information above is for the entire pan, not including chocolate chips. Cut into 6 pieces, each brownie is 45 calories.

Plant-based/Dairy-free option: Use dairy-free and/or plant-based protein powder.

Nut-free: Use nut-free milk instead of almond milk.

Sugar-free option: Use sugar-free syrup instead of maple syrup.

Easiest, Fudgiest 5-Ingredient Brownies

Serves 16

70 calories / 4 Fat / 5 g Net Carbs / 4 g Protein / 1 g Fiber / 3 g Sugar

INGREDIENTS:

½ cup cashew butter, or nut butter of choice (128 g)

½ cup unsweetened applesauce (90 g)

1½ scoops chocolate protein powder (42 g)

⅓ cup Dutch-process cocoa powder (30 g)

3 tablespoons coconut sugar (36 g)

Dark Chocolate Buttercream Frosting (page 168)

G Gluten-free

E Egg-free

G Grain-free

INSTRUCTIONS:

1. Preheat oven to 325°F. Line an 8x8-inch glass baking pan with parchment paper.
2. In a large bowl, combine nut butter and applesauce.
3. Add cocoa powder, protein powder, and coconut sugar, and mix until a thick batter forms.
4. Spread into parchment-lined pan.
5. Bake for 14 to 17 minutes.
6. Allow to cool, and frost with dark chocolate buttercream.
7. Slice into 12 pieces, and enjoy! Store in the refrigerator.

Plant-based/Dairy-free option: Use dairy-free and/or plant-based protein powder.

Nut-free option: Use sunflower-seed butter or coconut butter instead of nut butter.

Keto option: Use sugar-free sweetener instead of coconut sugar, and pumpkin or butter instead of applesauce. You may need to increase the amount of sweetener to ¼-½ cup – sweeten to taste.

Red Velvet Chocolate Chunk Brownies

Serves 8

91 calories / 4 g Fat / 8 g Net Carbs / 5 g Protein / 3.5 g Fiber / 4 g Sugar

INGREDIENTS:

¼ cup coconut flour (28 g)
¼ cup oat flour (30 g)
1 scoop vanilla whey protein powder (28 g)
¼ cup erythritol or baking stevia
2 tablespoons cocoa powder (10 g)
2 teaspoons ground flaxseed
½ teaspoon baking soda
¼ teaspoon salt
2 teaspoons maple syrup
2 teaspoons avocado oil
6 tablespoons unsweetened applesauce (90 g)
½ cup unsweetened almond milk (120 ml)
5–10 drops red food coloring (optional)
¼ cup dark chocolate chunks (60 g)
Cream Cheese Frosting I (page 191)

 Gluten-free
 Egg-free

INSTRUCTIONS:

1. Preheat oven to 350°F. Grease an 8x8-inch glass pan, or line with parchment paper.
2. Combine all dry ingredients (except chocolate chunks) in a mixing bowl. Add wet ingredients and stir just until combined. Fold in chocolate chunks.
3. Spread evenly into pan.
4. Bake for 17 to 22 minutes, until slightly firm in the center. Note that if you do not line your pan with parchment paper, you may need less baking time. You may also bake this recipe in four 5-inch ramekins to make jumbo red velvet cookie cakes.
5. Allow to cool, and slice into 8 pieces.
6. Frost individual brownies with cream cheese frosting immediately before serving. Enjoy!
7. Store in the refrigerator for freshness.

Plant-based/Dairy-free option: Use dairy-free and/or plant-based protein powder.

Nut-free option: Use nut-free milk instead of almond milk.

Sugar-free option: Use sugar-free sweetener instead of coconut sugar and use sugar-free chocolate chips.

Brownie Batter–Filled Cookie Cups

Serves 12

270 calories / 18.5 g Fat / 19 g Net Carbs / 7 g Protein / 5 g Fiber / 17 g Sugar

INGREDIENTS:

Cookie:

1 cup blanched almond flour (112 g)
½ cup coconut flour (56 g)
¼ cup coconut palm sugar (48 g)
6 tablespoons erythritol (72 g)
¼ teaspoon baking soda
½ teaspoon salt
6 tablespoons butter, softened (84 g)
2 tablespoons pure maple syrup (30 ml)
1 egg
½ teaspoon vanilla
½ cup mini chocolate chips (120 g)

Brownie Filling:

⅓ cup blanched almond flour (37 g)
1 scoop chocolate whey protein powder (28 g)
¼ cup Dutch-process cocoa powder (20 g)
¼ cup erythritol (48 g)
¼ teaspoon salt
½ cup unsweetened applesauce (120 g)
2 tablespoons pure maple syrup (30 ml)
2 teaspoons avocado oil
3 tablespoons mini chocolate chips (45 g)

Ⓖ Gluten-free
Ⓖ Grain-free

INSTRUCTIONS:

1. Preheat oven to 350°F. Grease 6 cups of a muffin tin and set aside.
2. Combine all dry cookie dough ingredients (aside from chocolate chips) in a large bowl.
3. Add wet ingredients and stir until dough forms. Fold in chocolate chips.
4. Divide cookie dough into two pieces: one piece will be two-thirds of the dough, and the other piece will be one-third. Divide each of these two pieces into 6 balls, then roll out each ball until about ⅛-inch thick. You will have 12 total flat round discs, and 6 of them will be larger than the remaining 6. Set aside.
5. Prepare brownie filling: add all dry ingredients to a bowl and stir until combined. Add wet ingredients, then fold in chocolate chips. Set aside.
6. Take your 6 larger cookie discs and place them into the muffin tin cups. Use your fingers to press them down until the muffin cup is fully lined with the cookie dough.
7. Distribute brownie batter evenly between the 6 cookie cups.
8. Now, take the 6 small cookie discs and place them on top of each cookie cup. Pinch the edges to attach the top cookie disc to the one that lines the muffin cup.
9. Bake for about 15 minutes.
10. Serve immediately for a lava cake effect! Each cup is quite large and rich, so they are best when cut in half and shared.

Dairy-free option: Use dairy-free butter and omit protein powder from brownie filling. Instead, increase almond flour in brownie filling to ½ cup.

Nut-free option: Use sunflower-seed flour instead of almond flour.

Sugar-free option: Use sugar-free sweetener instead of coconut sugar, sugar-free syrup, and sugar-free chocolate chips.

Small-Batch Brownies

Serves: 8

136 calories / 9.5 g Fat / 7 g Net Carbs / 5.5 g Protein / 2.5 g Fiber / 5.5 g Sugar

INGREDIENTS:

½ cup blanched almond flour (56 g)
2 tablespoons coconut flour (14 g)
¼ cup Dutch-process cocoa powder (20 g)
¾ scoop chocolate whey protein powder (21 g)
¼ cup erythritol (48 g)
1 teaspoon baking powder
¼ teaspoon salt
2 tablespoons avocado oil (30 ml)
2 tablespoons pure maple syrup (30 ml)
1 egg
2 tablespoons chocolate chips (30 g)

 Gluten-free
 Grain-free

INSTRUCTIONS:

1. Preheat oven to 350°F.
2. In a bowl, combine all dry ingredients (except chocolate chips).
3. Add oil, maple syrup, and egg, and stir until combined. Fold in chocolate chips.
4. Line an 8×4-inch baking dish with parchment paper, and spread batter evenly into pan.
5. Bake for 15 minutes.
6. Allow to cool before slicing and serving. Enjoy!

See these brownies on page 50.

Plant-based/Dairy-free option: Use dairy-free and/or plant-based protein powder.

Nut-free option: Use sunflower-seed flour or all-purpose gluten-free flour instead of almond flour.

Sugar-free option: Use sugar-free syrup instead of maple syrup and use sugar-free chocolate chips.

Super Fudgy Classic Brownies

Serves 16

75 calories / 2.5 g Fat / 8 g Net Carbs / 4 g Protein / 2 g Fiber / 4 g Sugar

INGREDIENTS:

1 large sweet potato, baked, skin removed
   (300 g after baking)

¼ cup unsweetened applesauce (60 g)

2 tablespoons coconut oil (28 g)

2 tablespoons unsweetened almond milk (30 ml)

1 teaspoon vanilla extract

2 scoops chocolate protein powder (56 g)

⅓ cup gluten-free quick oats (33 g)

½ cup Dutch-process cocoa powder (40 g)

2 tablespoons coconut sugar (24 g)

⅓ cup erythritol or baking stevia

2 tablespoons chocolate chips, melted (30 g)

½ teaspoon baking powder

¼ teaspoon baking soda

¼ teaspoon salt

INSTRUCTIONS:

1. Preheat oven to 325°F. Line an 8x8-inch glass baking pan with parchment paper.
2. In a food processor or high-speed blender (such as a Vitamix), blend sweet potato, applesauce, coconut oil, almond milk, and vanilla.
3. Add protein powder, quick oats, cocoa powder, coconut sugar, and stevia. Blend until combined.
4. Add chocolate, baking powder, baking soda, and salt, and blend just until combined.
5. Spread into parchment-lined pan.
6. Bake for 14 to 16 minutes.
7. Allow to cool.
8. Slice into 16 pieces, and enjoy! Store in the refrigerator for freshness.

Note: See the next page for how to make these into Triple-Layer Cookie Dough Brownies.

Plant-based/Dairy-free option: Use dairy-free and/or plant-based protein powder.

Nut-free option: Use nut-free milk instead of almond milk.

Sugar-free option: Use sugar-free sweetener instead of coconut sugar, and sugar-free chocolate chips.

Tips: I recommend underbaking these for best results; they may seem underdone when they first come out of the oven, but after setting and cooling, they will be perfectly firm and fudgy. Refrigerate for a few hours before enjoying for ultimate fudgy-ness.

Triple-Layer Cookie Dough Fudge Brownies

Serves 16

141 calories / 6 g Fat / 12 g Net Carbs / 7 g Protein / 3.5 g Fiber / 6.5 g Sugar

INGREDIENTS:

1 pan of Super Fudgy Classic Brownies (page 59)
1 recipe of Chocolate Buttercream Frosting
1 recipe of Edible Cookie Dough

Chocolate Buttercream Frosting:

½ scoop chocolate protein powder (14 g)
¼ cup cocoa powder (20 g)
¼ cup powdered erythritol or baking stevia
2 tablespoons unsweetened almond milk (30 ml)
2 teaspoons pure maple syrup
½ cup reduced-fat cream cheese (120 g)

Edible Cookie Dough:

6 tablespoons coconut flour (42 g)
½ scoop vanilla protein powder (14 g)
3 tablespoons baking stevia or erythritol
¼ teaspoon salt
¼ cup unsweetened applesauce (60 g)
¼ cup unsweetened almond milk (60 ml)
1½ tablespoons mini chocolate chips (22 g)

 Gluten-free
 Egg-free

INSTRUCTIONS:

1. Prepare brownies, and allow to cool in the refrigerator.
2. To make frosting, combine protein powder, cocoa powder, and stevia in a small bowl.
3. Add almond milk and maple syrup and stir until dry ingredients have dissolved.
4. Add cream cheese and stir until very smooth.
5. Spread frosting evenly over brownies, and return the pan to the refrigerator while preparing the cookie dough.
6. To make cookie dough, combine all dry ingredients (except chocolate chips) in a bowl. Add applesauce and almond milk and stir until a thick dough forms. Fold in chocolate chips.
7. Press cookie dough evenly on top of the buttercream frosting. Slice into 16 squares, and enjoy! Store in the refrigerator.

Note: Nutritional info for this recipe includes everything listed.

Dairy-free option: Use dairy-free protein powder, and dairy-free cream cheese.

Nut-free option: Use nut-free milk instead of almond milk.

Sugar-free option: Use sugar-free sweetener instead of coconut sugar.

Dark Chocolate Fudge Brownies

Serves: 16

155 calories / 9.5 g Fat / 15 g Net Carbs / 2 g Protein / 2 g Fiber / 7 g Sugar

INGREDIENTS:
¾ cup sweet white rice flour (120 g)
¼ cup tapioca starch (30 g)
½ cup Dutch-process cocoa powder (40 g)
¾ cup coconut palm sugar (144 g)
¼ teaspoon salt
½ cup refined coconut oil, melted (112 g)
2 eggs
1 teaspoon vanilla extract
¼ cup chocolate chips (60 g)

Ⓖ Gluten-free
Ⓓ Dairy-free
Ⓝ Nut-free

INSTRUCTIONS:
1. Preheat oven to 350°F.
2. In a large bowl, combine all dry ingredients (except chocolate chips).
3. Add coconut oil, and stir until distributed throughout dry ingredients.
4. Add eggs and vanilla extract and stir until combined. Fold in chocolate chips.
5. Line an 8x8-inch square glass pan with parchment paper, and spread batter evenly into pan.
6. Bake for 18 to 20 minutes.
7. Allow to cool. Slice and enjoy!

Sugar-free option: Use sugar-free sweetener instead of coconut sugar, and use sugar-free chocolate chips.

Keto Fudge Brownies

Serves 16

105 calories / 9.5 g Fat / 1.5 g Net Carbs / 2.5 g Protein / 3 g Fiber / 0 g Sugar

INGREDIENTS:

1 cup blanched almond flour (112 g)
⅓ cup Dutch-process cocoa powder (27 g)
2 tablespoons ground flaxseed (13 g)
½ cup erythritol (96 g)
1 teaspoon baking powder
¼ teaspoon salt
5 tablespoons butter, melted (70 g)
1 egg
⅓ cup sugar-free chocolate chips (80 g)

Ⓖ Gluten-free
Ⓚ Keto
Ⓢ Sugar-free
Ⓖ Grain-free

INSTRUCTIONS:

1. Preheat oven to 325°F. Line an 8x8-inch pan with parchment paper.
2. Combine all dry ingredients (except chocolate chips) in a large bowl, then add butter and egg.
3. Mix just until combined, then fold in chocolate chips.
4. Pour batter into pan and spread out evenly with the back of a spoon. Sprinkle top with extra chocolate chips, if desired.
5. Bake for 15 to 17 minutes.
6. Allow to cool.
7. Slice into 16 pieces. Enjoy!

Variation: Try adding 2 to 3 scoops of collagen protein powder to the dry ingredients for an extra boost of protein and health benefits. The collagen makes these brownies even more fudgy and chewy, so you may need to add a few minutes to the baking time.

Dairy-free option: Use dairy-free butter.

Creamy Mint Chocolate Brownies

Serves 16

72 calories / 3.5 g Fat / 5 g Net Carbs / 4 g Protein / 2 g Fiber / 3 g Sugar

INGREDIENTS:

½ cup gluten-free quick oats (40 g)
⅔ cup water (155 ml)
2 scoops chocolate whey protein powder (56 g)
3 tablespoons unsweetened almond milk (45 ml)
2 tablespoons coconut oil (28 g)
⅓ cup Dutch-process cocoa powder (30 g)
2 tablespoons pure maple syrup (30 ml)
⅓ cup baking stevia
2 teaspoons ground flaxseed
3 tablespoons chocolate chips (45 g)
¼ teaspoon baking soda
¼ teaspoon baking powder
¼ teaspoon salt
½ teaspoon mint extract
Creamy Mint Frosting (page 170)

G Gluten-free
E Egg-free

Plant-based/Dairy-free option: Use dairy-free and/or plant-based protein powder.

Nut-free option: Use nut-free milk instead of almond milk.

Sugar-free option: Use sugar-free sweetener instead of coconut sugar, and use sugar-free chocolate chips.

INSTRUCTIONS:

1. Preheat oven to 325°F.
2. Line an 8x8-inch glass baking pan with parchment paper.
3. Combine oats and water in a microwave-safe bowl (make sure the bowl is large enough that it will not overflow). Microwave for 1 minute, stir, then microwave for 1 more minute.
4. Add protein powder, almond milk, coconut oil, and cocoa powder and stir until combined.
5. Then stir in maple syrup, stevia, flax, and chocolate chips. Stir until chocolate chips are completely melted.
6. Add baking soda, baking powder, salt, and mint extract, and stir just until combined.
7. Spread into parchment-lined pan.
8. Bake for 13 to 16 minutes.
9. Allow to cool, and frost with Creamy Mint Frosting, if desired.
10. To make frosting, combine all ingredients in a small bowl and stir until combined. Spread evenly over cooled brownies.
11. Slice into 12 pieces and enjoy!

Tip! Refrigerate for a few hours after cooling for best results.

Cookie Dough–Filled Brownie Cups

Serves 8

115 calories / 3 g Fat / 11 g Net Carbs / 8 g Protein / 5 g Fiber / 4 g Sugar

INGREDIENTS:

1 large Japanese yam or other variety of white
   sweet potato, baked, skin removed (300 g is
   about 1¼ cups mashed; regular sweet potato can
   be substituted)
1 cup unsweetened applesauce (240 g)
1 tablespoon butter or coconut oil (14 g)
¼ cup unsweetened almond milk (60 ml)
1 teaspoon vanilla extract
2 scoops chocolate protein powder (56 g)
6 tablespoons coconut flour (42 g)
5 tablespoons Dutch-process cocoa powder (25 g)
2 teaspoons ground flaxseed
⅓ cup baking stevia or erythritol
1 teaspoon baking powder
¼ teaspoon salt
Edible Cookie Dough Filling (page 176)
Vanilla Cream Frosting and Filling (page 174)

G Gluten-free
E Egg-free
G Grain-free

INSTRUCTIONS:

1. Preheat oven to 350°F. Spray a cupcake tin
   with nonstick spray.
2. In a food processor or high-speed blender (such as
   a Vitamix), blend white sweet potato, applesauce,
   butter or coconut oil, almond milk, and vanilla.
3. Add protein powder, coconut flour, cocoa
   powder, flax, and stevia. Blend until combined.
4. Add baking powder and salt, and blend just until
   combined.
5. Divide into 8 cups.
6. Bake for 20 to 23 minutes.
7. Allow to cool.
8. Fill with cookie dough filling, if desired.
9. Slice a hole in the top of each brownie cup, and
   scoop out some of the center with a spoon.
   Divide cookie dough filling evenly. Use an icing
   bag to pipe vanilla frosting onto each brownie
   cup, if desired.
10. Enjoy! Store in the refrigerator.

Plant-based/Dairy-free option: Use dairy-free
and/or plant-based protein powder and dairy-free
yogurt.

Nut-free option: Use nut-free milk instead of
almond milk.

Sugar-free option: Use sugar-free sweetener instead
of coconut sugar, and use sugar-free chocolate chips.

Cheesecake Swirl Brownies

Serves 16

88 calories / 3 g Fat / 8.5 g Net Carbs / 5.5 g Protein / 2 g Fiber / 4 g Sugar

INGREDIENTS:

Brownies:

1 can white beans* (~240 g after draining and rinsing)

¼ cup unsweetened applesauce (60 g)

2 tablespoons butter or coconut oil (28 g)

¼ cup unsweetened almond milk (60 ml)

1 teaspoon vanilla extract

2 scoops chocolate protein powder (56 g)

¼ cup gluten-free quick oats (23 g)

⅓ cup Dutch-process cocoa powder (30 g)

3 tablespoons coconut sugar (36 g)

⅓ cup erythritol or baking stevia

3 tablespoons chocolate chips, melted (45 g)

½ teaspoon baking powder

¼ teaspoon baking soda

¼ teaspoon salt

Cheesecake Swirl:

¼ scoop vanilla protein powder (7 g)

1 tablespoon powdered erythritol

1 tablespoon unsweetened almond milk (15 ml)

¼ cup reduced-fat cream cheese (60 g)

*I used butter beans, but cannellini beans or navy beans will also work. These beans are extremely neutral in flavor; there is no flavor from the beans. Black beans can be used, but I find they can have a stronger flavor.

 Gluten-free

 Egg-free

INSTRUCTIONS:

1. Preheat oven to 325°F. Line an 8x8-inch glass baking pan with parchment paper.
2. In a food processor or high-speed blender (such as a Vitamix), blend drained and rinsed beans, applesauce, butter or oil, almond milk, and vanilla.
3. Add protein powder, oats, cocoa powder, coconut sugar, and stevia. Blend until combined.
4. Add chocolate, baking powder, baking soda, and salt, and blend just until combined.
5. Spread into parchment-lined pan.
6. To make cheesecake swirl, dissolve protein powder and stevia in almond milk. Add cream cheese and mix until smooth.
7. Pour cheesecake mixture over brownies, and use a knife to create a swirl pattern.
8. Bake for 17 to 20 minutes.
9. Allow to cool, slice into 16 pieces, and enjoy! Store in the refrigerator for freshness.

Plant-based/Dairy-free option: Use dairy-free and/or plant-based protein powder, and use dairy-free cream cheese.

Nut-free option: Use nut-free milk instead of almond milk.

Sugar-free option: Use sugar-free sweetener instead of coconut sugar, and use sugar-free chocolate chips.

Peanut Butter Swirl Fudge Brownies

Serves 12

84 calories / 4 g Fat / 6 g Net Carbs / 6 g Protein / 2 g Fiber / 3.5 g Sugar

INGREDIENTS:

½ cup gluten-free quick oats (40 g)
⅔ cup water (155 ml)
2 scoops chocolate whey protein powder (56 g)
3 tablespoons unsweetened almond milk (45 ml)
1 tablespoon coconut oil (14 g)
⅓ cup Dutch-process cocoa powder (27 g)
2 tablespoons pure maple syrup (30 ml)
⅓ cup erythritol or baking stevia
2 teaspoons ground flaxseed
2 tablespoons peanut butter (32 g), divided
3 tablespoons chocolate chips (45 g)
¼ teaspoon baking soda
¼ teaspoon baking powder
¼ teaspoon salt
Chocolate Peanut Butter Frosting (page 180)

Ⓖ Gluten-free
Ⓔ Egg-free

INSTRUCTIONS:

1. Preheat oven to 325°F. Line 8x8-inch glass baking pan with parchment paper.
2. Combine oats and water in a microwave-safe bowl (make sure the bowl is large enough that it will not overflow). Microwave for 1 minute, stir, then microwave for 1 more minute.
3. Add protein powder, almond milk, coconut oil, and cocoa powder, and stir until combined.
4. Next, stir in maple syrup, stevia, flax, one tablespoon of the peanut butter, and chocolate chips. Stir until chocolate chips are completely melted.
5. Add baking soda, baking powder, and salt, and stir just until combined. Swirl remaining tablespoon of peanut butter into the batter— stir very gently, do not completely combine.
6. Spread into parchment-lined pan.
7. Bake for 13 to 16 minutes.
8. Allow to cool. Frost with Chocolate Peanut Butter Frosting and top with a drizzle of peanut butter, if desired.

Plant-based/Dairy-free option: Use dairy-free and/or plant-based protein powder.

Nut-free option: Use nut-free milk instead of almond milk, and use sunflower-seed butter instead of peanut butter.

Sugar-free option: Use sugar-free syrup instead of maple syrup, and use sugar-free chocolate chips.

Red Velvet Brownies

Serves: 12

88 calories / 2 g Fat / 9 g Net Carbs / 6 g Protein / 4.5 g Fiber / 5 g Sugar

INGREDIENTS:

½ can white beans (~120 g after draining and rinsing)
4 small cooked beets (190 g)
¾ cup unsweetened applesauce (180 g)
1 tablespoon butter or coconut oil (14 g)
¼ cup unsweetened almond milk (60 ml)
1 teaspoon apple cider vinegar
1 teaspoon vanilla extract
2 scoops vanilla whey protein powder (56 g)
⅓ cup coconut flour (38 g)
2 tablespoons cocoa powder (10 g)
1 tablespoon coconut sugar (12 g)
2 teaspoons ground flaxseed
⅓ cup erythritol or baking stevia
¼ teaspoon baking soda
¼ teaspoon salt
5–10 drops natural or regular red food coloring (optional)

Ⓖ Gluten-free
Ⓔ Egg-free
Ⓖ Grain-free

INSTRUCTIONS:

1. Preheat oven to 325°F. Line an 8x8-inch glass baking pan with parchment paper.
2. In a food processor or high-speed blender (such as a Vitamix), blend drained and rinsed beans, beets, applesauce, butter or oil, almond milk, vinegar, and vanilla.
3. Add protein powder, coconut flour, flax, and stevia. Blend until combined.
4. Add baking soda, salt, and food coloring, and blend just until combined.
5. Spread into parchment-lined pan.
6. Bake for 17 to 22 minutes.
7. Allow to cool, slice into 12 pieces, and enjoy!
8. Store in the refrigerator.

Plant-based/Dairy-free option: Use dairy-free and/or plant-based protein powder.

Nut-free option: Use nut-free milk instead of almond milk.

Sugar-free option: Use sugar-free sweetener instead of coconut sugar.

Magic Brownies

Serves 12

92 calories / 3.5 g Fat / 6 g Net Carbs / 9 g Protein / 2 g Fiber / 5 g Sugar

INGREDIENTS:

3 scoops chocolate whey protein powder (84 g)

3 tablespoons coconut flour (21 g)

½ cup Dutch-process cocoa powder (40 g)

¼ cup coconut sugar (48 g)

⅓ cup erythritol or baking stevia

2 teaspoons ground flax

¼ teaspoon baking soda

¼ teaspoon baking powder

¼ teaspoon salt

3 tablespoons butter or coconut oil, melted (42 g)

1 cup nonfat plain Greek yogurt (227 g)

½ cup unsweetened almond milk (120 ml)

½ teaspoon vanilla extract

2 tablespoons mini chocolate chips (30 g, optional; not included in nutritional information)

Chocolate Protein Frosting (see page 164)

Chocolate Ganache (see page 150)

INSTRUCTIONS:

1. Preheat oven to 325°F. Line an 8x8-inch glass baking pan with parchment paper.
2. Combine protein powder, coconut flour, cocoa powder, coconut sugar, stevia, flax, baking soda, baking powder, and salt in a large mixing bowl.
3. Add butter or oil, yogurt, almond milk, and vanilla. Mix just until combined.
4. Fold in chocolate chips, if desired.
5. Spread into parchment-lined pan.
6. Bake for 17 to 20 minutes.
7. Allow to cool.
8. Frost with Chocolate Protein Frosting or Chocolate Ganache, if desired.
9. Slice and enjoy! Store in the refrigerator.

G Gluten-free

E Egg-free

G Grain-free

Plant-based/Dairy-free option: Use dairy-free and/or plant-based protein powder, and replace Greek yogurt with applesauce.

Fudge Brownie Donuts

Serves 6

137 calories / 6 g Fat / 12.5 g Net Carbs / 7 g Protein / 5 g Fiber / 5.5 g Sugar

INGREDIENTS:

⅓ cup coconut flour (37 g)
1 scoop chocolate whey protein powder (28 g)
¼ cup Dutch-process cocoa powder (20 g)
2 tablespoons gluten-free oat flour (15 g)
2 tablespoons tapioca starch (15 g)
1 tablespoon coconut palm sugar (12 g)
½ teaspoon baking soda
¼ teaspoon salt
⅓ cup baking stevia or erythritol
2 teaspoons ground flaxseed meal
1 tablespoon avocado oil (15 ml)
½ cup unsweetened applesauce (120 g)
1 teaspoon vanilla extract
½ cup unsweetened almond milk or brewed
coffee (120 ml)
2 tablespoons chocolate chips (30 g)

G Gluten-free
E Egg-free

INSTRUCTIONS:

1. Preheat oven to 350°F. In a large bowl, combine all dry ingredients (except chocolate chips).
2. Add oil, pumpkin or applesauce, and vanilla.
3. Pour in almond milk or coffee and stir until a thick batter consistency is reached. Do not overmix. Fold in chocolate chips.
4. Spray a standard-sized donut pan with nonstick spray, and evenly distribute the batter into six donuts. Smooth out each donut with the back of a spoon.
5. Bake for 15 to 17 minutes.
6. Allow to cool and top with frosting of choice. Enjoy!

Plant-based/Dairy-free option: Use dairy-free and/or plant-based protein powder.

Nut-free option: Use nut-free milk instead of almond milk.

Sugar-free option: Use sugar-free sweetener instead of coconut sugar, and use sugar-free chocolate chips.

Chocolate Chip Cookie Blondies, page 94

Blondies

Chocolate Chip Cheesecake Bars

Serves: 16

185 Calories 13.5 g Fat / 9 g Net Carbs / 5.5 g Protein / 2 g Fiber / 8.5 g Sugar

INGREDIENTS:

Cookie Layer:
1 cup blanched almond flour (112 g)
¼ cup coconut flour (28 g)
¼ cup coconut sugar (48 g)
¼ cup erythritol (48 g)
½ teaspoon baking soda
½ teaspoon salt
3 tablespoons butter, softened (42 g)
1 egg
1 teaspoon vanilla extract
½ cup chocolate chips (120 g)

Cheesecake Layer:
1 cup cream cheese, room temperature (227 g)
1 scoop vanilla whey protein powder (28 g)
¼ cup powdered erythritol (48 g)
1 tablespoon pure maple syrup (15 ml)
1 egg
½ teaspoon vanilla extract

 Gluten-free
 Grain-free

INSTRUCTIONS:

1. Preheat oven to 350°F. Grease an 8x8-inch square baking dish, or line with parchment paper.
2. Make cookie layer: combine dry ingredients (except chocolate chips) in a large bowl. Add softened butter, egg, and vanilla. Fold in chocolate chips.
3. Press two-thirds of the cookie dough evenly into the bottom of the pan. Reserve remaining cookie dough.
4. Make cheesecake layer: combine all ingredients in a bowl and beat on medium speed until smooth.
5. Pour cheesecake mixture into the pan on top of the cookie dough.
6. Form remaining cookie dough into flat disc shapes and distribute on top of cheesecake mixture.
7. Bake for 25 minutes.
8. Allow to cool completely, then refrigerate for at least 1 hour before slicing and serving.
9. Store in the refrigerator.

Dairy-free option: Use dairy-free butter and dairy-free cream cheese, and omit protein powder.

Nut-free option: Use all-purpose gluten-free flour instead of almond flour.

Keto option: Use sugar-free sweetener, sugar-free syrup, and sugar-free chocolate chips.

Keto Chocolate Chip Cookie Squares

Serves: 16

101 Calories / 9 g Fat / 1.8 g Net Carbs / 2.5 g Protein / 2.5 g Fiber / 0.3 g Sugar

INGREDIENTS:

1 cup blanched almond flour (112 g)
½ cup powdered erythritol (96 g)
¼ teaspoon baking soda
½ teaspoon salt
5 tablespoons butter, softened (70 g)
1 egg
1 teaspoon vanilla extract
½ cup sugar-free chocolate chips (120 g)

G Gluten-free
K Keto
S Sugar-free
G Grain-free

INSTRUCTIONS:

1. Preheat oven to 350°F. Grease an 8x8-inch square baking dish, or line with parchment paper.
2. Combine dry ingredients (except chocolate chips) in a large bowl.
3. Add softened butter, egg, and vanilla extract, and stir until combined.
4. Fold in chocolate chips.
5. Spread batter evenly into baking dish, and top with a few extra chocolate chips, if desired.
6. Bake for 27 to 30 minutes, until lightly golden brown on the edges.
7. Allow to cool, slice, and enjoy!

Dairy-free option: Use dairy-free butter.

Double-Layer Funfetti Blondie

Serves 4

64 Calories / 2 g Fat / 5.5 g Net Carbs / 3 g Protein / 2 g Fiber / 1 g Sugar

INGREDIENTS:
2 tablespoons gluten-free oat flour (15 g)
2 tablespoons coconut flour (14 g)
⅓ scoop vanilla- or birthday-cake-flavored protein powder (21 g)
1 tablespoon tapioca starch (8 g)
2 tablespoons erythritol or baking stevia
1 teaspoon ground flaxseed
¼ teaspoon baking powder
⅛ teaspoon salt
1 teaspoon avocado oil or melted coconut oil
3 tablespoons unsweetened applesauce (45 g)
¼ cup unsweetened almond milk (60 ml)
2 teaspoons sprinkles (8 g; optional)
Cream Cheese Frosting III (page 194)

Ⓖ Gluten-free
Ⓢ Sugar-free
Ⓔ Egg-free

INSTRUCTIONS:
1. Preheat oven to 325°F. Spray two 5-inch round ramekins with nonstick spray.
2. Combine all dry ingredients (except sprinkles) in a small bowl.
3. Add oil, applesauce, and almond milk. Mix just until combined.
4. Fold in sprinkles.
5. Divide batter evenly into each ramekin, and bake for about 15 minutes.
6. Allow to cool. Frost one layer with cream cheese frosting, stack the other layer on top, then continue to frost until both layers are covered.
7. Slice into four pieces and enjoy!
8. Store in the refrigerator.

Plant-based/Dairy-free option: Use dairy-free and/or plant-based protein powder.

Nut-free option: Use nut-free milk instead of almond milk.

Brown Butter Blondies

Serves: 16

135 Calories / 11 g Fat / 4.5 g Net Carbs / 3 g Protein / 1 g Fiber / 4.5 g Sugar

INGREDIENTS:

½ cup butter (112 g)
⅓ cup coconut sugar (64 g)
½ cup erythritol (96 g)
2 eggs
1 teaspoon vanilla
1⅓ cup blanched almond flour (150 g)
½ teaspoon baking powder
½ teaspoon salt
Vanilla Whipped Cream (page 186)

 Gluten-free
 Grain-free

INSTRUCTIONS:

1. Preheat oven to 350°F. Grease an 8x8-inch baking dish, or line with parchment paper.
2. Cook butter in a saucepan over low-medium heat for about minutes, stirring constantly, until light brown with a nutty aroma. Be careful not to burn the butter.
3. Pour slightly cooled brown butter into a large bowl and add sweeteners, eggs, and vanilla. Whisk to combine.
4. Combine dry ingredients in a separate bowl.
5. Pour dry into wet, and stir just until combined.
6. Bake for 30 to 35 minutes (baking time may need to be decreased if pan is not lined with parchment). Allow to cool before slicing.
7. Enjoy! Serve with Vanilla Whipped Cream, if desired.

Dairy-free option: Use dairy-free butter.

Nut-free option: Use sunflower-seed flour instead of almond flour.

Keto option: Use sugar-free sweetener instead of coconut sugar.

Keto "Brookies"
(brownie + cookie bars)

Serves 16

170 calories / 15.5 g Fat / 2.5 g Net Carbs / 4.5 g Protein / 4 g Fiber / 1 g Sugar

INGREDIENTS:

Cookie Layer:
1⅓ cups blanched almond flour (150 g)
⅓ cup erythritol (64 g)
½ teaspoon baking soda
¼ teaspoon salt
¼ cup butter, softened (56 g)
1 egg
½ teaspoon vanilla
⅓ cup sugar-free chocolate chips (80 g)

Brownie Layer:
⅔ cup blanched almond flour (74 g)
½ cup erythritol (96 g)
¼ cup cocoa powder (20 g)
½ teaspoon baking powder
¼ teaspoon salt
3 tablespoons butter, softened (42 g)
1 egg
3 tablespoons sugar-free chocolate chips (45 g)

Ⓖ Gluten-free
Ⓚ Keto
Ⓖ Grain-free
Ⓢ Sugar-free

INSTRUCTIONS:

1. Preheat oven to 350°F. Line an 8x8-inch square pan with parchment paper.
2. Start with cookie layer: combine dry ingredients (except chocolate chips) in a large bowl. Add butter and stir until distributed. Add egg and vanilla and stir until combined. Fold in chocolate chips.
3. Spoon about ⅔ of the cookie dough into the bottom of the pan. Use wet fingers to spread dough evenly over bottom of pan.
4. Follow same instructions as cookie layer to assemble brownie ingredients.
5. Spoon brownie batter into the pan, and use either the back of a spoon or wet fingers to spread brownie batter evenly over cookie dough.
6. Take remaining ⅓ of cookie dough and distribute randomly on top of brownie batter. I formed the remaining dough into circle shapes to keep some brownie peeking through.
7. Bake for 25 to 30 minutes.
8. Allow to cool, slice, and enjoy!

> **Dairy-free option:** Use dairy-free butter.
>
> **Nut-free option:** Use sunflower-seed flour instead of almond flour.

Chocolate Chip Cookie Blondies

Serves 16

96 calories / 5 g Fat / 7.5 g Net Carbs / 5 g Protein / 2 g Fiber / 4 g Sugar

INGREDIENTS:

1 (15-oz) can white beans, drained and rinsed
   (~250 g after draining and rinsing)
¼ cup gluten-free oats (28 g)
¼ cup applesauce (60 g)
¼ cup grass-fed butter or coconut oil (56 g)
2 scoops vanilla whey protein powder (56 g)
¼ cup erythritol or baking stevia
1 tablespoon coconut palm sugar (12 g)
1 teaspoon baking powder
¼ teaspoon salt
1 teaspoon vanilla extract
6 tablespoons chocolate chips (90 g)

G Gluten-free
N Nut-free
E Egg-free

INSTRUCTIONS:

1. Preheat oven to 325°F.
2. Add beans, oats, applesauce, and butter/coconut oil to a high-speed blender or food processor. Blend until combined.
3. Add the remaining ingredients (except chocolate chips) and blend until very smooth.
4. Fold in chocolate chips.
5. Spray an 8x8-inch glass pan with nonstick spray, or line with parchment paper. Spoon in the batter, and smooth out with the back of a spoon.
6. Bake for 13 to 15 minutes, being very careful not to overbake. Blondies should still appear slightly underdone.
7. Allow to cool completely before slicing and serving. Refrigerating will help them to set sooner. Store covered in the refrigerator for up to 3 to 4 days (if they last that long!).

Plant-based/Dairy-free option: Use dairy-free and/or plant-based protein powder.

Sugar-free option: Use sugar-free sweetener instead of coconut sugar, and use sugar-free chocolate chips.

Sugar Cookie Blondies

Serves 12

57 calories / 2 g Fat / 4 g Net Carbs / 4 g Protein / 1 g Fiber / 1 g Sugar

INGREDIENTS:
¼ cup gluten-free oat flour (30 g)
¼ cup coconut flour (28 g)
1½ scoops vanilla whey protein powder (42 g)
2 tablespoons tapioca starch (15 g)
¼ cup erythritol or baking stevia
1 teaspoon ground flaxseed
½ teaspoon baking powder
⅛ teaspoon salt
2 tablespoons butter or coconut oil, melted (28 g)
6 tablespoons unsweetened applesauce (90 g)
¼ cup unsweetened almond milk (60 ml)
½ teaspoon vanilla extract
Cream Cheese Frosting IV (page 195)

(G) Gluten-free
(S) Sugar-free
(E) Egg-free

INSTRUCTIONS:
1. Preheat oven to 325°F. Line an 8x8-inch glass baking pan with parchment paper.
2. Combine all dry ingredients in a large mixing bowl. Add butter or oil, applesauce, almond milk, and vanilla. Mix just until combined.
3. Spread into parchment-lined pan.
4. Bake for 17 minutes.
5. Allow to cool, and spread with cream cheese frosting.
6. Slice into 12 pieces, and enjoy! Store in the refrigerator.

Plant-based/Dairy-free option: Use dairy-free and/or plant-based protein powder, and use dairy-free butter or coconut oil.

Nut-free option: Use nut-free milk instead of almond milk.

White Chocolate Blondies

Serves 12

93 calories / 3 g Fat / 9 g Net Carbs / 5 g Protein / 2 g Fiber / 3 g Sugar

INGREDIENTS:

1 large Japanese yam or other variety of white sweet potato, baked, skin removed (300 g, or about 1¼ cups mashed)

½ cup unsweetened applesauce (120 g)

2 tablespoons butter or coconut oil (28 g)

2 tablespoons unsweetened almond milk (30 ml)

1 teaspoon vanilla extract

2 scoops whey vanilla protein powder (56 g)

½ cup gluten-free quick oats (42 g)

2 tablespoons coconut flour (14 g)

2 teaspoons ground flaxseed

2 tablespoons white chocolate chips, melted (30 g)

1 teaspoon baking powder

¼ teaspoon salt

Salted Caramel Buttercream Frosting (page 171)

G Gluten-free

E Egg-free

INSTRUCTIONS:

1. Preheat oven to 350°F. Line an 8x8-inch glass baking pan with parchment paper.
2. In a food processor or high-speed blender, blend white sweet potato, applesauce, butter or coconut oil, almond milk, and vanilla.
3. Add protein powder, oatmeal, coconut flour, flax, and melted white chocolate. Blend until combined.
4. Add baking powder and salt, and blend just until combined.
5. Spread into parchment-lined pan.
6. Bake for 20 to 25 minutes.
7. Allow to cool, and top with Salted Caramel Buttercream Frosting, if desired.
8. Slice and enjoy! Store in the refrigerator.

Plant-based/Dairy-free option: Use dairy-free and/or plant-based protein powder.

Nut-free option: Use nut-free milk instead of almond milk.

Sugar-free option: Use sugar-free white chocolate, or omit and sweeten to taste with sugar-free sweetener.

Birthday Cake Blondie Cups

Serves 8

102 calories / 2.5 g Fat / 9 g Net Carbs / 8 g Protein / 3.5 g Fiber / 2.8 g Sugar

INGREDIENTS:

1 large Japanese yam or other variety of white sweet potato, baked, skin removed (300 g, or about 1¼ cups mashed)

1 cup unsweetened applesauce (240 g)

1 tablespoon butter or coconut oil (14 g)

¼ cup unsweetened almond milk (60 ml)

1 teaspoon vanilla extract

2 scoops vanilla- or birthday-cake-flavored whey protein powder (56 g)

6 tablespoons coconut flour (42 g)

2 teaspoons ground flaxseed

3 tablespoons erythritol or baking stevia

1 teaspoon baking powder

¼ teaspoon salt

2 tablespoons sprinkles (optional)

Vanilla Cream Frosting and Filling (page 174)

G Gluten-free
S Sugar-free
E Egg-free
G Grain-free

INSTRUCTIONS:

1. Preheat oven to 350°F. Spray a cupcake tin with nonstick spray.
2. In a food processor or high-speed blender, blend white sweet potato, applesauce, butter or coconut oil, almond milk, and vanilla.
3. Add protein powder, coconut flour, flax, and stevia. Blend until combined.
4. Add baking powder and salt, and blend just until combined. Fold in sprinkles, if desired.
5. Divide into 8 cups.
6. Bake for 20 to 23 minutes.
7. Allow to cool and then, or fill with vanilla cream filling if desired.

To fill: Slice a hole in the top of each blondie cup, and scoop out some of the center with a spoon. Divide filling evenly between blondie cups, overflowing it a bit to cover the top as well. You can pipe filling using a plastic sandwich bag with a corner cut out, or just spoon the filling in and spread with a knife. Enjoy! Store in the refrigerator.

Plant-based/Dairy-free option: Use dairy-free and/or plant-based protein powder.

Nut-free option: Use nut-free milk instead of almond milk.

Cinnamon Bun Collagen Breakfast Bars

Serves: 9

145 calories / 7.5 g Fat / 14 g Net Carbs / 5.5 g Protein / 1 g Fiber / 5 g Sugar

INGREDIENTS:

1½ cups gluten-free quick oats (144 g)
3 scoops collagen protein (30 g)
⅓ cup coconut sugar (64 g)
¼ teaspoon salt
1 teaspoon baking powder
1 teaspoon cinnamon
Pinch of ginger, nutmeg, or spices of choice
½ cup unsweetened almond milk (120 ml)
¼ cup avocado oil, melted coconut oil,
    or dairy-free butter (56 g)
1 egg
1 teaspoon vanilla extract

G Gluten-free
D Dairy-free

INSTRUCTIONS:

1. Preheat oven to 350°F. Line an 8x8-inch inch pan with parchment paper.
2. Add all dry ingredients to a large bowl and stir.
3. Add wet ingredients and whisk until combined.
4. Spread batter evenly into pan.
5. Bake for 20 to 22 minutes or until slightly firm in the center.
6. Allow to cool, and slice into 9 pieces.
7. Enjoy cold or warmed up. Pictured here, topped with dairy-free coconut yogurt and cinnamon.

Tip! Try drizzling with melted coconut butter for a healthy icing, or serve warm with vanilla ice cream for an extra treat. (It tastes like apple crisp without the apples!)

Plant-based option: Omit collagen protein, and replace egg with ¼ cup unsweetened applesauce or mashed banana. Vegetarian option: omit collagen protein.

Nut-free option: Use nut-free milk instead of almond milk.

Sugar-free option: Use sugar-free sweetener instead of coconut sugar.

Peanut Butter & Jelly Blondies

Serves 8

113 calories / 6.5 g Fat / 9 g Net Carbs / 4 g Protein / 1 g Fiber / 6 g Sugar

INGREDIENTS:

Blondie Layer:
½ scoop vanilla protein powder (14 g)
2 tablespoons coconut flour (14 g)
2 teaspoons powdered peanut butter
1 tablespoon tapioca starch (8 g)
2 tablespoons baking stevia
2 teaspoons ground flax
¼ teaspoon baking powder
⅛ teaspoon salt
¼ cup + 1 tablespoon unsweetened almond milk (75 ml)

Peanut Butter Layer:
5 tablespoons peanut butter (80 g)
2 teaspoons coconut oil (10 g)

Additional:
⅓ cup raspberry jam (100 g)

G Gluten-free
E Egg-free
G Grain-free

INSTRUCTIONS:

1. Preheat oven to 325°F. Line a 7x5-inch glass pan with parchment paper.
2. Combine protein powder, coconut flour, powdered peanut butter, starch, stevia, flax, baking powder, and salt in a bowl.
3. Add almond milk and stir until a dough forms.
4. Spread evenly into parchment-lined pan.
5. Bake for 8 to 12 minutes.
6. Allow to cool.
7. Melt coconut oil and combine with peanut butter. Depending on the texture of your peanut butter, you may have to warm it up a bit.
8. Pour peanut butter mixture evenly over the blondie layer, and place in the refrigerator to solidify for 20–30 minutes.
9. Remove from refrigerator and spread evenly with raspberry jam. Return to refrigerator to set for 30 minutes.
10. Slice and enjoy! Store covered in the refrigerator, or freeze if desired.

Plant-based/Dairy-free option: Use dairy-free and/or plant-based protein powder.

Nut-free option: Use nut-free milk instead of almond milk, and use sunflower-seed butter instead of peanut butter.

Sugar-free option: Use sugar-free jam.

Magic Bars

Serves 16

188 calories / 11 g Fat / 16 g Net Carbs / 6 g Protein / 3 g Fiber / 9 g Sugar

INGREDIENTS:

Crust:
1⅓ cups gluten-free oat flour (160 g)
½ cup gluten-free oats (40 g)
¼ teaspoon salt
6 tablespoons coconut oil (84 g)
2 tablespoons pure maple syrup (30 ml)

Filling:
1½ scoops vanilla protein powder (42 g)
⅓ cup unsweetened almond milk (80 ml)
3 tablespoons ground flaxseed (20 g)
2 tablespoons pure maple syrup (30 ml)
½ teaspoon vanilla extract
1 egg white
2 scoops collagen protein powder (optional, not included in nutritional information)

Add-ins:
⅔ cup chocolate chips (160 g)
⅓ cup chopped walnuts or pecans (34 g)
¼ cup unsweetened shredded coconut (12 g)
Pinch sea salt

Ⓖ Gluten-free

INSTRUCTIONS:

1. Preheat oven to 350°F. Line an 8x8-inch glass pan with parchment paper.
2. Combine oat flour, oats, and salt in a bowl.
3. Add coconut oil and maple syrup, and stir until a thick dough forms.
4. Press dough evenly into the bottom of the pan.
5. Add protein powder to a separate bowl. Add almond milk slowly until protein powder dissolves, then add remaining almond milk.
6. Add flax, maple syrup, vanilla, egg white, and optional collagen to the milk/protein mixture. Stir until smooth, then allow to sit for 5 to 10 minutes to thicken.
7. Pour milk mixture into the pan. Distribute half of the chocolate chips and half of the nuts evenly on top of the mixture. Sprinkle coconut evenly over the chocolate chips and nuts, then distribute the remaining chocolate and nuts. Press everything down gently with your fingers or a fork. Sprinkle a pinch of sea salt on top, if desired.
8. Bake for 22 to 25 minutes.
9. Allow to cool completely. Slice into 16 bars and enjoy! Store at room temperature for up to 2 days, or refrigerate up to a week.

Dairy-free option: Use dairy-free and/or plant-based protein powder.

Nut-free option: Use nut-free milk instead of almond milk.

Sugar-free option: Use sugar-free syrup instead of maple syrup, but keep in mind the crust may not hold together as well.

Cookies & Cookie Dough

The Best Plant-Based Chocolate Chip Cookies

Serves: 12

167 Calories / 10.5 g Fat / 17 g Net Carbs / 2 g Protein / 2 g Fiber / 14 g Sugar

INGREDIENTS:

½ cup gluten-free all-purpose flour (74 g)
½ cup blanched almond flour (56 g)
¼ cup coconut sugar (48 g)
½ teaspoon baking soda
½ teaspoon salt
5 tablespoons dairy-free butter, softened (70 g)
¼ cup pure maple syrup (60 ml)
½ teaspoon vanilla extract
½ cup dairy-free chocolate chips (120 g)

G Gluten-free
P Plant-based
D Dairy-free
E Egg-free

INSTRUCTIONS:

1. Combine all dry ingredients (except chocolate chips) in a large bowl.
2. Add butter, maple syrup, and vanilla. Stir until a thick dough forms.
3. Fold in chocolate chips.
4. Dough will be very sticky. Transfer dough to refrigerator to chill for at least 30 minutes to 1 hour before baking.
5. Preheat oven to 350°F. Form into 12 balls and place on parchment-lined cookie sheet. Flatten each ball slightly.
6. Bake for 7 to 9 minutes.
7. Allow to cool and then enjoy!

Note: These may be the best plant-based cookies, but some have said they are the best cookies ever—plant-based and gluten-free, or not!

Nut-free option: replace almond flour with gluten free all-purpose flour or sunflower-seed flour.

Lower sugar option: replace coconut sugar with a sugar-free sweetener, and use sugar-free chocolate chips.

Double Chocolate Cookies

Serves 12

110 calories 10 g F / 1.5 g C (net) / 3 g P / 3 g fiber / 0.3 g sugar

INGREDIENTS:

¾ cup blanched almond flour (84 g)
2 tablespoons ground flax (13 g)
⅓ cup Dutch-process cocoa powder (27 g)
½ cup erythritol (96 g)
¼ teaspoon baking soda
¼ teaspoon salt
¼ cup butter, softened (56 g)
1 egg
¼ cup sugar-free chocolate chips (60 g)

Chocolate Icing:
6 tablespoons powdered erythritol (72 g)
2 tablespoons cocoa powder (10 g)
2 tablespoons water (30 ml)

(G) Gluten-free
(K) Keto
(S) Sugar-free
(G) Grain-free

INSTRUCTIONS:

1. Preheat oven to 350°F. Line a cookie sheet with parchment paper.
2. Combine all dry ingredients (except chocolate chips) in a large bowl, then add softened butter and egg.
3. Mix until combined, then fold in chocolate chips.
4. Allow dough to rest for 5 to 10 minutes before spooning heaping tablespoons of dough onto lined cookie sheet. If you'd like smoother cookies (as pictured), use damp fingers to smooth out each dough ball, then flatten.
5. Bake for 6 to 8 minutes.
6. Make chocolate icing if desired: combine powdered erythritol + cocoa powder in a small bowl. Add water slowly until desired consistency is reached.
7. Frost cooled cookies and enjoy!

Dairy-free option: Use dairy-free butter.

Nut-free option: Use sunflower-seed flour instead of almond flour.

Gooey, Chewy Chocolate Chip Cookies

Serves 12

160 calories 14.5 g F / 2 g C (net) / 4 g P / 4.5 g fiber / 0.5 g sugar

INGREDIENTS:

1¼ cups blanched almond flour (140 g)
2 tablespoons ground flax (13 g)
½ cup erythritol (96 g)
¼ teaspoon baking soda
½ teaspoon salt
¼ cup butter, softened (56 g)
2 tablespoons cream cheese (30 g)
1 egg
1 teaspoon vanilla extract
½ cup sugar-free chocolate chips (120 g)

Ⓖ Gluten-free
Ⓚ Keto
Ⓢ Sugar-free
Ⓖ Grain-free

INSTRUCTIONS:

1. Preheat oven to 350°F. Line a cookie sheet with parchment paper.
2. Combine all dry ingredients (except chocolate chips) in a large bowl, then add softened butter and cream cheese, egg, and vanilla.
3. Mix until combined, then fold in chocolate chips.
4. Allow dough to rest for 5 to 10 minutes before spooning heaping tablespoons of dough onto lined cookie sheet.
5. Bake for 12 to 14 minutes.
6. Allow to cool and enjoy!

Note: This recipe makes 12 large cookies. If making smaller cookies, decrease baking time as needed.

Dairy-free option: Use dairy-free butter.

Nut-free option: Use sunflower-seed flour instead of almond flour.

Sugar Cookies

Serves 15

99 Calories / 8.5 g Fat / 1 g Net Carbs / 2.5 g Protein / 1.7 g Fiber / 0.5 g Sugar

INGREDIENTS:

¼ cup unsalted butter, room temperature (56 g)
1 egg
½ teaspoon vanilla extract
1¼ cup blanched almond flour (140 g)
¼ cup coconut flour (28 g)
¾ cup powdered erythritol (144 g)
½ teaspoon baking powder
¼ teaspoon salt
Sugar Cookie Buttercream Icing (page 188)

Tip: Regular powdered sugar may be used if you do not need the cookies to be sugar-free or keto.

Ⓖ Gluten-free
Ⓚ Keto
Ⓢ Sugar-free
Ⓖ Grain-free

> **Dairy-free option:** Use dairy-free butter.
>
> **Nut-free option:** Use sunflower-seed flour instead of almond flour.

INSTRUCTIONS:

1. Preheat oven to 350°F. Line a cookie sheet with parchment paper.
2. Combine room-temperature butter, egg, and vanilla in a bowl and beat until smooth.
3. In a separate bowl, combine all dry ingredients.
4. Add dry ingredients to wet, and stir until a dough forms.
5. Form dough into one big ball and allow to rest for about 30 minutes at room temperature or in the refrigerator for easier rolling.
6. To roll out the dough, sprinkle powdered sweetener on a large piece of parchment or wax paper, then place the dough on top. Top dough with more sweetener and another piece of parchment or wax paper.
7. Roll the dough sandwiched between the paper to desired thickness (minimum ¼ inch thick).
8. Cut dough into desired shapes using cookie cutters. To create these circle shapes, I used the rim of a wineglass.
9. Use a spatula to transfer shapes onto cookie sheet, and bake for about 10 minutes. Baking time may vary depending on the shape and size of your cookies.
10. Allow to cool, and frost with Sugar Cookie Buttercream Icing on page 188, if desired. Enjoy!

Chocolate Chip Skillet Cookie

Serves 8

183 calories / 9 g Fat / 14 g Net Carbs / 9 g Protein / 3 g Fiber / 9 g Sugar

INGREDIENTS:

⅔ cup gluten-free quick oats (60 g)
1 cup water (240 ml)
¼ cup unsweetened almond milk (60 ml)
2 scoops vanilla whey protein powder (56 g)
1 tablespoon ground flax (7 g)
3 tablespoons butter or coconut oil (42 g)
¼ cup coconut flour (28 g)
3 tablespoons coconut sugar (36 g)
¼ teaspoon baking soda
¼ teaspoon baking powder
¼ teaspoon salt
1 teaspoon vanilla extract
⅓ cup chocolate chips (80 g)

G Gluten-free
E Egg-free

INSTRUCTIONS:

1. Preheat oven to 350°F. Grease a 10-inch cast-iron skillet, or line a round baking pan with parchment paper.
2. Combine oats and water in a microwave-safe bowl (make sure the bowl is large enough so that the oats will not spill over). Microwave for 1 minute, stir, then microwave for 1 more minute. Add almond milk, protein powder, flax, and butter. Stir until protein dissolves and butter has melted.
3. Add coconut flour, sugar, baking soda, baking powder, salt, and vanilla.
4. Allow to cool for a few minutes if batter is still very warm, then gently fold in chocolate chips. Spread evenly into pan.
5. Bake for about 13 minutes.
6. Allow to cool and enjoy!

Plant-based/Dairy-free option: Use dairy-free and/or plant-based protein powder, and use dairy-free butter or coconut oil.

Nut-free option: Use nut-free milk instead of almond milk.

Sugar-free option: Use sugar-free sweetener instead of coconut sugar.

Jumbo Chocolate Chip Protein Cookies

Serves 2

105 calories / 3 g Fat / 9 g Net Carbs / 6 g Protein / 4 g Fiber / 4.5 g Sugar

INGREDIENTS:

1½ tablespoons gluten-free oat flour (10 g)
2 tablespoons coconut flour (14 g)
⅓ scoop vanilla whey protein powder (9 g)
1½ tablespoons erythritol or baking stevia
½ teaspoon ground flaxseed
⅛ teaspoon baking soda
⅛ teaspoon salt
3 tablespoons unsweetened applesauce (45 g)
1 tablespoon unsweetened almond milk (15 ml)
½ teaspoon vanilla extract
2 teaspoons mini chocolate chips

 Gluten-free
 Egg-free

INSTRUCTIONS:

1. Preheat oven to 350°F. Line a baking sheet with parchment paper.
2. Combine all dry ingredients (except chocolate chips) in a large mixing bowl. Add applesauce, almond milk, and vanilla. Mix until a dough forms.
3. Add one teaspoon of the chocolate chips to the cookie dough, and form into two large cookies in desired thickness (about 3.5 inches in diameter), as they won't spread much while baking. Top with remaining chocolate chips.
4. Bake for 6 to 10 minutes.
5. Allow to cool and then enjoy!

Plant-based/Dairy-free option: Use dairy-free and/or plant-based protein powder.

Nut-free option: Use nut-free milk instead of almond milk.

Sugar-free option: Use sugar-free chocolate chips.

Jumbo White Chocolate Macadamia Protein Cookies

Serves 4

125 calories / 5.5 g Fat / 9 g Net Carbs / 6 g Protein / 4 g Fiber / 5 g Sugar

INGREDIENTS:

3 tablespoons gluten-free oat flour (22 g)
¼ cup coconut flour (28 g)
⅓ scoop vanilla whey protein powder (9 g)
3 tablespoons stevia
1 teaspoon ground flaxseed
¼ teaspoon baking soda
¼ teaspoon salt
6 tablespoons unsweetened applesauce (90 g)
3 tablespoons unsweetened almond milk (45 ml)
1 tablespoon white chocolate chips (15 g)
2 tablespoons macadamia nuts, chopped (14 g)

G Gluten-free
E Egg-free

INSTRUCTIONS:

1. Preheat oven to 350°F. Line a baking sheet with parchment paper.
2. Combine all dry ingredients (except chocolate chips and macadamia nuts) in a large mixing bowl. Add applesauce and almond milk. Mix until a dough forms.
3. Add about one teaspoon of the white chocolate chips and one tablespoon of the macadamia nuts to the cookie dough, and mix until combined.
4. Form into four large cookies in desired thickness (about 3.5 inches in diameter), as they won't spread much while baking.
5. Top with remaining white chocolate chips and macadamia nuts.
6. Bake for 6 to 10 minutes.
7. Allow to cool and then enjoy!

Plant-based/Dairy-free option: Use dairy-free and/or plant-based protein powder and white chocolate chips.

Nut-free option: Use nut-free milk instead of almond milk.

Sugar-free option: Use sugar-free white chocolate chips or omit.

Jumbo Double-Chocolate Fudge Brownie Cookies

Serves 2

104 calories 3g F / 9g C (net) / 6.5g P / 4g fiber / 5g sugar

INGREDIENTS:

1½ tablespoons gluten-free oat flour (10 g)
2 tablespoons coconut flour (14 g)
⅓ scoop chocolate whey protein powder (9 g)
1 tablespoon Dutch-process cocoa powder (5 g)
2 tablespoons erythritol or baking stevia
½ teaspoon ground flaxseed
⅛ teaspoon baking soda
⅛ teaspoon salt
3 tablespoons unsweetened applesauce (45 g)
2 tablespoons unsweetened almond milk (30 ml)
½ teaspoon vanilla extract
2 teaspoons mini chocolate chips

G Gluten-free
E Egg-free

INSTRUCTIONS:

1. Preheat oven to 325°F. Line a baking sheet with parchment paper.
2. Combine all dry ingredients (except chocolate chips) in a large mixing bowl. Add applesauce, almond milk, and vanilla. Mix until a dough forms.
3. Add 1 teaspoon of the chocolate chips to the cookie dough, and form into two large cookies in desired thickness (about 3.5 inches in diameter), as they won't spread much while baking. Top with remaining chocolate chips.
4. Bake for 6 to 10 minutes.
5. Allow to cool and then enjoy!

Plant-based/Dairy-free option: Use dairy-free and/or plant-based protein powder.

Nut-free option: Use nut-free milk instead of almond milk.

Sugar-free option: Use sugar-free chocolate chips.

Jumbo Peanut Butter–Filled Fudge Brownie Cookies

Serves 2

135 calories 6g F / 10g C (net) / 8g P / 4.5g fiber / 5g sugar

INGREDIENTS:

1½ tablespoons gluten-free oat flour (10 g)
2 tablespoons coconut flour (14 g)
⅓ scoop chocolate whey protein powder (9 g)
1 tablespoon Dutch-process cocoa powder (5 g)
2 tablespoons stevia
½ teaspoon ground flaxseed
⅛ teaspoon baking soda
⅛ teaspoon salt
3 tablespoons unsweetened applesauce (45 g)
2 tablespoons unsweetened almond milk (30 ml)
½ teaspoon vanilla extract
2 teaspoons mini chocolate chips
2 teaspoons peanut butter

G Gluten-free
E Egg-free

INSTRUCTIONS:

1. Preheat oven to 325°F. Line a baking sheet with parchment paper.
2. Combine all dry ingredients (except chocolate chips) in a large mixing bowl. Add applesauce, almond milk, and vanilla. Mix until a dough forms.
3. Add 1 teaspoon of the chocolate chips to the cookie dough, and form into two large cookies in desired thickness (about 3.5 inches in diameter), as they won't spread much while baking. Reserve two smaller balls of dough.
4. Using your fingers, create a well in the middle of each cookie. Fill each well with 1 teaspoon of peanut butter.
5. Take the two reserved balls of dough, flatten them, and use them to cover the wells of peanut butter. Use your fingers to seal the cookies.
6. Top with remaining chocolate chips.
7. Bake for 6 to 10 minutes.
8. Allow to cool and then enjoy!

Plant-based/Dairy-free option: Use dairy-free and/or plant-based protein powder.

Nut-free option: Use nut-free milk instead of almond milk, and use sunflower-seed butter instead of peanut butter.

Sugar-free option: Use sugar-free chocolate chips.

Flourless Fudge Cookies

Serves 6

56 Calories / 1 g Fat / 7 g Net Carbs / 4 g Protein / 1 g Fiber / 3 g Sugar

INGREDIENTS:

Cookie:

¾ scoop chocolate whey protein powder (21 g)

3 tablespoons Dutch-process cocoa powder (15 g)

2 teaspoons coconut sugar

1 tablespoon ground flax (6 g)

¼ cup baking stevia

¼ teaspoon baking powder

⅛ teaspoon salt

2 teaspoons mini chocolate chips (optional, not included in nutritional information)

½ cup mashed sweet potato (120 g)

Chocolate Fudge Frosting **(adds 9 calories per cookie):**

2 tablespoons cocoa powder (10 g)

2 stevia packets, or about 1½ tablespoons powdered sweetener of choice

1 teaspoon pure maple syrup

1 tablespoon water (15 ml)

Ⓖ Gluten-free

Ⓝ Nut-free

Ⓔ Egg-free

Ⓖ Grain-free

INSTRUCTIONS:

1. Preheat oven to 325°F. Line a baking sheet with parchment paper.
2. Combine all dry ingredients in a mixing bowl.
3. Add sweet potato and stir until a dough forms.
4. Spoon dough into 6 cookies on parchment-lined baking sheet.
5. Bake for 6 to 10 minutes.
6. Allow to cool, and frost with chocolate fudge frosting, if desired.
7. To make frosting, combine cocoa and stevia in a small bowl. Add maple syrup and water, and stir until smooth.
8. Store cookies in the refrigerator.

Plant-based/Dairy-free option: Use dairy-free and/or plant-based protein powder.

Sugar-free option: Use sugar-free sweetener instead of coconut sugar. Sweeten to taste.

Hot Chocolate Fudge Cookies

Serves 4

96 calories / 3.8 g Fat / 8 g Net Carbs / 5 g Protein / 4 g Fiber / 4 g Sugar

INGREDIENTS:

3 tablespoons coconut flour (21 g)
2 tablespoons all-purpose gluten-free flour (18 g)
½ scoop chocolate whey protein powder (14 g)
¼ cup baking stevia
2 tablespoons Dutch-process cocoa powder (10 g)
1 teaspoon ground flaxseed
¼ teaspoon baking soda
⅛ teaspoon salt
1 teaspoon pure maple syrup
1 teaspoon avocado oil or coconut oil
5 tablespoons pumpkin puree (75 g)
1 tablespoon + 1 teaspoon unsweetened almond milk (20 ml)
1 tablespoon chocolate chips (15 g)

G Gluten-free
E Egg-free

INSTRUCTIONS:

1. Preheat oven to 350°F. Line a baking sheet with parchment paper.
2. Combine all dry ingredients (except chocolate chips) in a mixing bowl.
3. Add wet ingredients and stir until a thick dough forms.
4. Add chocolate chips.
5. Form dough into four balls and flatten to desired thickness. Place on a parchment paper–lined baking sheet and top each cookie with extra chocolate chips if desired.
6. Bake for 6 to 8 minutes, being careful not to overbake. The cookies should still be slightly underdone in the center.
7. Allow to cool and then enjoy!

Pictured layered with Peanut Butter Cookie Dough from page 40 and natural peanut butter.

Plant-based/Dairy-free option: Use dairy-free and/or plant-based protein powder.

Nut-free option: Use nut-free milk instead of almond milk.

Sugar-free option: Use sugar-free syrup instead of maple syrup, and use sugar-free chocolate chips.

Oil-Free Chocolate Chip Cookies

Serves 4

76 calories / 2.5 g Fat / 10 g Net Carbs / 2 g Protein / 1.5 g Fiber / 5 g Sugar

INGREDIENTS:

2 tablespoons coconut flour (14 g)
3 tablespoons tapioca starch (22 g)
¼ scoop vanilla protein powder (7 g)
2 tablespoons erythritol or baking stevia
⅛ teaspoon baking soda
⅛ teaspoon salt
3 tablespoons unsweetened applesauce (45 g)
2 tablespoons chocolate chips (30 g)

G Gluten-free
N Nut-free
E Egg-free
G Grain-free

INSTRUCTIONS:

1. Preheat oven to 350°F. Line a baking sheet with parchment paper.
2. Combine all dry ingredients (except chocolate chips) in a mixing bowl.
3. Add applesauce and stir until a thick dough forms.
4. Add chocolate chips.
5. Form dough into four balls and flatten to desired thickness.
6. Place on a parchment paper lined–baking sheet.
7. Bake for 5 to 7 minutes, being careful not to overbake. The cookies should still appear slightly underdone in the center.
8. Allow to cool and enjoy!

Plant-based/Dairy-free option: Use dairy-free and/or plant-based protein powder.

Sugar-free option: Use sugar-free chocolate chips.

Plant-Based Cookie Dough

Serves 11

76 calories / 3 g Fat / 10 g Net Carbs / 1 g Protein / 2 g Fiber / 5 g Sugar

INGREDIENTS:

6 tablespoons coconut flour (42 g)

¼ cup tapioca starch (30 g)

2 tablespoons erythritol or baking stevia

¼ teaspoon salt

2 teaspoons ground flax

1 tablespoon dairy-free butter or coconut oil, melted (14 g)

¼ cup pure maple syrup (60 ml)

3 tablespoons unsweetened applesauce (45 g)

½ teaspoon vanilla extract

3 tablespoons chocolate chips (45 g)

G Gluten-free

N Nut-free

P Plant-based

D Dairy-free

E Egg-free

G Grain-free

INSTRUCTIONS:

1. Combine coconut flour, starch, sweetener, salt, and ground flax in a mixing bowl.
2. Add butter or oil, maple syrup, applesauce, and vanilla.
3. Stir until a thick dough forms, then fold in chocolate chips.
4. Form into 11 balls, and enjoy!
5. Store in an airtight container the refrigerator or freezer for freshness.

Tip! For an extra-decadent cookie dough, substitute the applesauce for extra dairy-free butter or coconut oil.

Sugar-free option: Use sugar-free syrup instead of maple syrup, and use sugar-free chocolate chips.

Chocolate Chip Cookie Dough Sandwich

Serves: 2

226 calories / 11 g Fat / 22 g Net Carbs / 9 g Protein / 4 g Fiber / 10 g Sugar

INGREDIENTS:

1 serving of chocolate ganache* (page 39)
1 recipe Classic Chocolate Chip Cookies
1 tablespoon almond butter (16 g)

Classic Chocolate Chip Cookies:

1½ tablespoons coconut flour (10 g)
2 tablespoons tapioca or arrowroot starch (15 g)
⅓ scoop vanilla whey protein powder (9 g)
2 teaspoons coconut palm sugar
1/16 teaspoon (pinch) baking soda
⅛ teaspoon salt
1 teaspoon coconut oil, melted
2 tablespoons applesauce (30 g)
⅛ teaspoon vanilla extract
1 tablespoon mini chocolate chips (15 g)

G Gluten-free
E Egg-free
G Grain-free

INSTRUCTIONS:

1. Prepare chocolate ganache the night before.
2. Combine all dry cookie dough ingredients in a small bowl.
3. Add coconut oil and distribute throughout dry ingredients.
4. Add remaining ingredients and stir until a dough forms.
5. Form half the dough into two cookies.
6. Bake at 350°F for 7 to 10 minutes.
7. Allow to cool.
8. Flip one cookie over, and top with the remaining unbaked dough.
9. Spread with chocolate ganache and almond butter, and top with the other cookie. Slice in half, and enjoy!

*1 serving of chocolate ganache is equivalent to ¼ serving of the 5-Ingredient Flourless Chocolate Fudge Cake with Chocolate Ganache, unbaked, on page 39.

Note: Nutritional information for this recipe includes everything listed.

Plant-based/Dairy-free option: Use dairy-free and/or plant-based protein powder.

Nut-free option: Use sunflower-seed butter instead of almond butter.

Sugar-free option: Use sugar-free sweetener instead of coconut sugar.

Pumpkin Spice Cheesecake-Filled Cookies

Serves 9

90 calories / 3 g Fat / 9 g Net Carbs / 4.5 g Protein / 2 g Fiber / 4.5 g Sugar

INGREDIENTS:

Cookies:

½ cup gluten-free all-purpose flour (74 g)

¼ cup coconut flour (28 g)

1 scoop vanilla protein powder (28 g)

¼ teaspoon baking powder

¼ teaspoon baking soda

1 teaspoon ground flaxseed

1 teaspoon cinnamon

1 teaspoon pumpkin pie spice

3 tablespoons erythritol or baking stevia

½ cup pumpkin puree (120 g)

2 teaspoons avocado oil

2 tablespoons maple syrup (30 ml)

Cheesecake Filling:

¼ cup reduced-fat cream cheese (56 g)

2 tablespoons powdered erythritol or stevia

¼ teaspoon vanilla extract

G Gluten-free

N Nut-free

E Egg-free

INSTRUCTIONS:

1. Preheat oven to 350°F. Line a baking sheet with parchment paper.
2. Mix all dry ingredients in a large bowl.
3. Add wet ingredients and stir until dough forms.
4. Form in 9 balls and flatten.
5. Mix cheesecake filling ingredients in a small bowl.
6. Top each cookie with a dollop of the mixture. Fold the cookies around the filling, and place on a parchment-lined baking sheet.
7. Bake for 10 to 15 minutes.
8. Allow to cool and then enjoy!
9. Store in the refrigerator.

Plant-based/Dairy-free option: Use dairy-free and/or plant-based protein powder, and use dairy-free cream cheese.

Sugar-free option: Use sugar-free syrup instead of maple syrup.

Keto Pumpkin Chocolate Chip Cookies

Serves 12

145 calories / 13 g Fat / 2.5 g Net Carbs / 4.5 g Protein / 4.5 g Fiber / 1 g Sugar

INGREDIENTS:

3 tablespoons pumpkin puree (45 g)
2 tablespoons grass-fed butter, softened (28 g)
2 tablespoons cream cheese, softened (28 g)
1 egg
½ teaspoon vanilla extract
1½ cups blanched almond flour (168 g)
½ cup erythritol (96 g)
½ teaspoon pumpkin pie spice
¼ teaspoon baking soda
½ teaspoon salt
½ cup sugar-free chocolate chips (112 g)

Ⓖ Gluten-free
Ⓚ Keto
Ⓢ Sugar-free
Ⓖ Grain-free

INSTRUCTIONS:

1. Preheat oven to 350°F. Line a cookie sheet with parchment paper.
2. In a large bowl, combine pumpkin, softened butter and cream cheese, egg, and vanilla.
3. In a separate bowl, combine the dry ingredients (except chocolate chips).
4. Pour the dry ingredients into the wet ingredients, and stir until combined.
5. Fold in the chocolate chips.
6. Drop heaping tablespoons of dough onto cookie sheet, and flatten a bit, as the cookies will not spread much while baking. If you want the outside of the cookies to be perfectly smooth, use slightly damp fingers to smooth them out.
7. Bake for 12 to 14 minutes.
8. Allow to cool and then enjoy!

Dairy-free option: Use dairy-free butter and cream cheese.

Nut-free option: Use sunflower-seed flour instead of almond flour.

Cookie Dough Cheesecake Dessert Dip

Serves 13

105 calories / 7.5g Fat / 9 g Net Carbs / 2 g Protein / 0 g Fiber / 8 g Sugar

INGREDIENTS:
1 cup cream cheese (227 g)
1 tablespoon butter or ghee (14 g)
¼ cup coconut palm sugar (48 g)
1 teaspoon vanilla extract
¼ teaspoon salt
⅓ cup chocolate chips (80 g)
Optional add-ins/variations (not included in nutritional information or allergen icons): collagen protein powder, nut butter, cocoa powder, a few tablespoons of gluten-free oat flour for more of a dough texture, white chocolate or peanut butter chips, sprinkles, etc.

G Gluten-free
N Nut-free
E Egg-free
G Grain-free

INSTRUCTIONS:
1. In a bowl with electric mixer, mix cream cheese and butter/ghee until combined.
2. Add coconut sugar, vanilla, and salt, and mix until very smooth. If adding protein powder or nut butter (optional add-ins), add those and mix again until smooth.
3. Fold in chocolate chips.
4. Spoon mixture into a serving bowl, and serve with gluten-free pretzels, chips, fruit, or anything else your heart desires! For a thicker texture, refrigerate for an hour or two before serving. Enjoy!

Dairy-free option: Use dairy-free butter and cream cheese.

Keto/sugar-free option: Use sugar-free sweetener instead of coconut sugar, and use sugar-free chocolate chips.

Red Velvet Donut Cake Pops, page 150

Whoopie Pies, Fudge, Truffles & More

Keto Cookie Dough Fudge

Serves 12

175 Calories / 16 g Fat / 4.5 g Net Carbs / 3 g Protein / 4.5 g Fiber / 1 g Sugar

INGREDIENTS:

½ cup grass-fed butter, softened (112 g)
½ cup smooth cashew butter (128 g)
⅔ cup sugar-free sweetener of choice
6 tablespoons coconut flour (42 g)
½ teaspoon salt
1 teaspoon vanilla
½ cup sugar-free chocolate chips (120 g)

Note: I tested 2 different versions: one with ⅓ cup granulated erythritol and ⅓ cup baking stevia, and one with ⅓ cup powdered erythritol and ⅓ cup baking stevia. I find that granulated erythritol does not dissolve well in cold recipes, so if you want a very smooth texture, use powdered. I loved both versions and didn't mind the slight crunchy texture of the granulated erythritol. Make sure to sweeten to taste, as different sweeteners add different amounts of sweetness.

INSTRUCTIONS:

1. Line an 8x4-inch loaf pan with parchment or wax paper.
2. Combine softened butter and cashew butter in a bowl.
3. Add coconut flour, salt, and vanilla.
4. Add ⅓ cup of sweetener, then slowly add the rest of the sweetener to taste.
5. Stir in 2 to 3 tablespoons of the chocolate chips.
6. Spread mixture into an 8x4 inch loaf pan.
7. Top generously with remaining chocolate chips, and add extra if desired.
8. Refrigerate or freeze until firm, then slice into 12 pieces! Enjoy!
9. Store in the refrigerator.

Ⓖ Gluten-free
Ⓚ Keto
Ⓢ Sugar-free
Ⓔ Egg-free
Ⓖ Grain-free

Plant-based/Dairy-free option: Use dairy-free butter and chocolate chips.

Nut-free option: Use sunflower-seed butter instead of cashew butter.

Rice Crispy Treats

Serves: 9

80 Calories / 3.5 g Fat / 9 g Net Carbs / 3 g Protein / 0 g Fiber / 6 g Sugar

INGREDIENTS:

3 tablespoons salted butter (42 g)
¼ cup pure maple syrup (60 ml)
1 scoop vanilla whey protein powder (28 g)
2 cups gluten-free puffed-rice cereal (60 g)

Ⓖ Gluten-free
Ⓝ Nut-free
Ⓔ Egg-free

INSTRUCTIONS:

1. Line an 8x8-inch pan with parchment paper.
2. Melt butter in a saucepan over low heat.
3. Add maple syrup and stir for a minute until syrup heats up.
4. Remove from heat and quickly add protein powder. Stir until a thick, sticky sauce forms, then add puffed rice, and stir quickly to completely coat all the cereal.
5. Press mixture evenly into the parchment-lined pan, add any desired toppings, and allow to cool. Slice into bars. Enjoy!

Plant-based/Dairy-free option: Use dairy-free butter and protein powder. Note that consistency may not be the same when using nondairy-based protein powders.

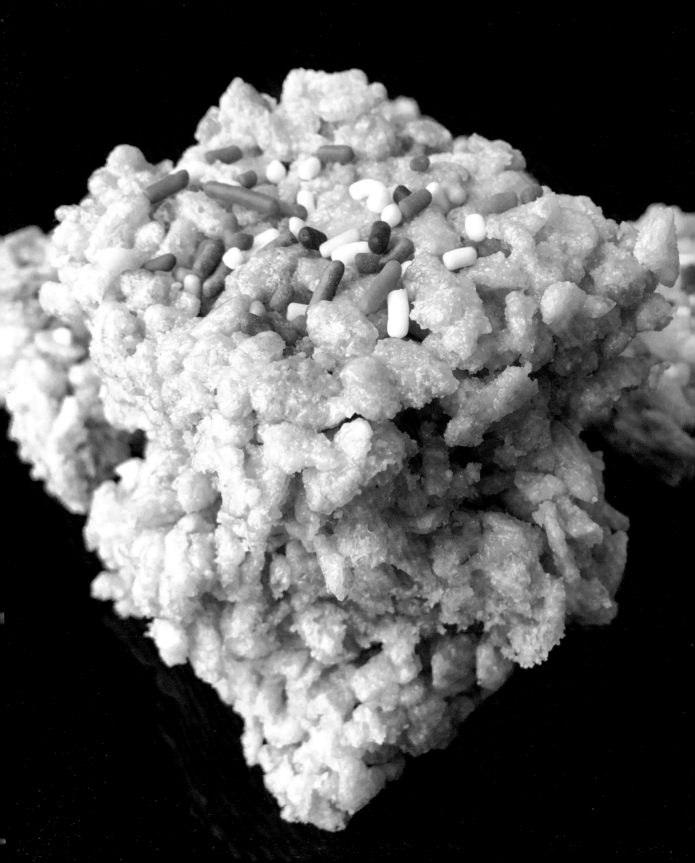

Red Velvet Donut Cake Pops

Serves 15

102 calories / 6 g Fat / 7.5 g Net Carbs / 4 g Protein / 2.5 g Fiber / 5.5 g Sugar

INGREDIENTS:

Donuts:

6 tablespoons coconut flour (42 g)
¼ cup gluten-free oat flour (28 g)
1 scoop vanilla whey protein powder (28 g)
1 tablespoon cocoa powder (5 g)
½ teaspoon baking soda
¼ teaspoon salt
¼ cup baking stevia
2 teaspoons ground flaxseed meal
1 tablespoon avocado oil or melted butter (14 g)
1 tablespoon pure maple syrup (15 ml)
6 tablespoons unsweetened applesauce (90 g)
½ cup unsweetened almond milk (120 ml)
1 teaspoon apple cider vinegar
1 teaspoon vanilla extract
5–10 drops red food coloring, optional

Frosting:

½ cup plain Greek yogurt (120 g)
1½ tablespoons honey (31 g)

Chocolate Ganache:

⅓ cup coconut oil (80 g)
⅓ cup chocolate chips (80 g)
½ cup cocoa powder (40 g)

Ⓖ Gluten-free
Ⓔ Egg-free

INSTRUCTIONS:

1. Preheat oven to 350°F.
2. Combine all dry donut ingredients in a large bowl.
3. Add wet ingredients, and stir gently just until combined.
4. Distribute batter six ways in a greased standard-sized donut pan.
5. Bake for about 15 minutes.
6. Allow donuts to cool, then remove from pan and place into a large bowl.
7. Use hands to crumble donuts into a medium to fine crumb.
8. In a separate bowl, combine frosting ingredients and mix until smooth.
9. Add frosting to the crumbled donut mixture, and stir until a thick ball of dough forms.
10. Form the dough into 15 balls, and pierce each one with a lollipop stick.
11. Make the chocolate ganache by combining coconut oil and chocolate chips in a double boiler, stirring constantly until chocolate chips are melted. Remove from heat.
12. Add cocoa powder, and stir until smooth.
13. Take each cake pop one at a time, and cover completely in the chocolate ganache.
14. Before the chocolate hardens, dip into sprinkles or other toppings, if desired.
15. Place on a sheet of wax paper, and repeat with all remaining cake pops.

16. Place donut pops in the freezer to set for 20 to 30 minutes before serving, or store them in the freezer and remove one hour before serving. Enjoy!

Note: You will only use about two-thirds of the chocolate ganache, and the nutritional information reflects this. However, you will have trouble coating the last few pops if you do not make the full amount. Pour the leftover ganache into a bowl lined with wax paper and refrigerate to harden, then enjoy as a chocolate bar!

Plant-based/Dairy-free option: Use plant-based/dairy-free protein powder, and dairy-free yogurt.

Nut-free option: Use nut-free milk instead of almond milk.

Sugar-free option: Use sugar-free syrup instead of maple syrup or honey, and use sugar-free chocolate chips.

Brownie Cookie Dough Truffles

Serves 11

38 calories / 2 g Fat / 3 g Net Carbs / 1 g Protein / 1 g Fiber / 2 g Sugar

INGREDIENTS:

¼ cup coconut flour (28 g)
2 tablespoons Dutch-process cocoa powder (10 g)
3 tablespoons erythritol or baking stevia
2 tablespoons peanut butter (32 g)
1 tablespoon + 1 teaspoon pure maple syrup
 (20 ml)
3 tablespoons unsweetened almond milk (45 ml)
Pinch salt, to taste
1 tablespoon mini chocolate chips (15 g; optional,
 not included in nutritional information)

Ⓖ Gluten-free
Ⓟ Plant-based
Ⓓ Dairy-free
Ⓔ Egg-free
Ⓖ Grain-free

INSTRUCTIONS:

1. Combine coconut flour, cocoa powder, and stevia in a small bowl.
2. Add peanut butter and maple syrup.
3. Slowly add almond milk until a thick dough forms. Add salt to taste.
4. Fold in chocolate chips, if desired.
5. Form into 11 balls, and enjoy!
6. Store covered in the refrigerator, or freeze to be enjoyed at a later date.

Nut-free option: Use nut-free milk instead of almond milk, and use sunflower-seed butter instead of peanut butter.

Sugar-free option: Use sugar-free syrup instead of maple syrup, and use sugar-free chocolate chips.

Chocolate-Covered Peanut Butter Cookie Dough Truffles

Serves 15

45 calories / 2.5 g Fat / 3 g Net Carbs / 2 g Protein / 1 g Fiber / 2 g Sugar

INGREDIENTS:

¼ cup coconut flour (28 g)
¼ cup powdered peanut butter (24 g)
2 teaspoons erythritol or baking stevia
1 teaspoon ground flax
⅛ teaspoon salt
2 tablespoons peanut butter (32 g)
1 tablespoon pure maple syrup (15 ml)
¼ cup unsweetened almond milk (60 ml)

Chocolate Coating:

1⅔ tablespoons chocolate chips (25 g)
1½ teaspoons coconut oil
1 tablespoon cocoa (5 g)

G Gluten-free
P Plant-based
D Dairy-free
E Egg-free
G Grain-free

INSTRUCTIONS:

1. Combine dry ingredients in a small bowl.
2. Add peanut butter and maple syrup. Slowly add almond milk until a thick dough forms.
3. Form into 15 balls. Place in the refrigerator while preparing chocolate coating.
4. Melt chocolate chips and coconut oil together, then add cocoa powder.
5. Coat each peanut butter ball evenly in chocolate. Place on wax paper and allow to harden in the refrigerator.
6. Store covered in the refrigerator, or freeze to be enjoyed at a later date. Enjoy!

Sugar-free option: Use sugar-free syrup instead of maple syrup, and use sugar-free chocolate chips.

Chocolate Chip Cookie Dough Whoopie Pie

Serves 2

155 calories / 4 g Fat / 14 g Net Carbs / 11 g Protein / 5 g Fiber / 9 g Sugar

INGREDIENTS:

2 Jumbo Chocolate Chip Protein Cookies (page 120)
1 recipe of Cookie Dough Frosting

Cookie Dough Frosting:
5 tablespoons nonfat plain Greek yogurt (75 g)
1 tablespoon coconut flour (7 g)
1 teaspoon coconut sugar
½ teaspoon mini chocolate chips

G Gluten-free
N Nut-free
E Egg-free

INSTRUCTIONS:

1. Prepare cookies and allow them to cool.
2. Combine yogurt, coconut flour, and coconut sugar in a small bowl. Add chocolate chips.
3. Flip one cookie over and spread with frosting. Cover with other cookie.
4. Roll sides in mini chocolate chips, if desired.
5. Slice in half, and enjoy!

Note: Nutritional information for this recipe includes everything listed.

Plant-based/Dairy-free option: Use dairy-free cream cheese or yogurt instead of regular Greek yogurt, and follow substitution instructions for the cookies.

Sugar-free option: Use sugar-free sweetener instead of coconut sugar, and use sugar-free chocolate chips.

Fudge Brownie Whoopie Pie

Serves 2

140 calories / 3.5 g Fat / 11 g Net Carbs / 11 g Protein / 5 g Fiber / 6.5 g Sugar

INGREDIENTS:

2 Jumbo Double-Chocolate Fudge Brownie
  Cookies (page 124)
1 recipe of Vanilla Cream Frosting

Vanilla Cream Frosting:
5 tablespoons nonfat plain Greek yogurt (75 g)
1 tablespoon coconut flour (7 g)
2 teaspoons powdered erythritol or baking stevia
¼ teaspoon vanilla extract

Ⓖ Gluten-free
Ⓢ Sugar-free
Ⓔ Egg-free

INSTRUCTIONS:

1. Prepare cookies and allow to cool.
2. Combine yogurt, coconut flour, stevia, and vanilla in a small bowl.
3. Flip one cookie over and spread with frosting. Cover with other cookie.
4. Slice in half, and enjoy!

Note: Nutritional information for this recipe includes everything listed.

Plant-based/Dairy-free: Use dairy-free yogurt or cream cheese in frosting, and follow substitution instructions for the cookies.

White Chocolate Macadamia Vanilla Cream Whoopie Pie

Serves 2

160 calories / 6 g Fat / 11 g Net Carbs / 10.5 g Protein / 5 g Fiber / 6.5 g Sugar

INGREDIENTS:

2 Jumbo White Chocolate Macadamia Protein Cookies (page 123)
1 recipe Vanilla Cream Frosting

Vanilla Cream Frosting
5 tablespoons nonfat plain Greek yogurt (75 g)
1 tablespoon coconut flour (7 g)
2 teaspoons powdered erythritol or baking stevia
¼ teaspoon vanilla extract

G Gluten-free
S Sugar-free
E Egg-free

INSTRUCTIONS:

1. Prepare cookies and allow to cool.
2. Combine yogurt, coconut flour, sweetener, and vanilla in a small bowl.
3. Flip one cookie over and spread with frosting. Cover with other cookie.
4. Slice in half, and enjoy!

Note: Nutritional information for this recipe includes everything listed.

Plant-based/Dairy-free: Use dairy-free yogurt or cream cheese in frosting, and prepare cookies according to dairy-free instructions.

Keto Peanut Butter Cup Fat Bombs

Serves 4

224 calories / 21 g Fat / 6.5 g Net Carbs / 5 g Protein / 8 g Fiber / 3 g Sugar

INGREDIENTS:

5 ounces sugar-free 55% cacao dark chocolate*
  (141 g)
2 teaspoons coconut oil
3 tablespoons unsweetened peanut butter (48 g)
1 tablespoon powdered erythritol (12 g)
Pinch fine-ground salt (optional)

Ⓖ Gluten-free
Ⓚ Keto
Ⓢ Sugar-free
Ⓔ Egg-free
Ⓖ Grain-free

*I used a 55% cacao chocolate bar sweetened with stevia and erythritol. You may use any sugar-free chocolate bar, however, I do not recommend using 100% unsweetened baking chocolate.

Note: This recipe makes four very large peanut butter cups. You may use mini cupcake liners to make smaller cups, or cut each cup in half for a smaller serving.

INSTRUCTIONS:

1. Place 4 standard-sized cupcake liners on a small plate, or use a silicone mold.
2. Melt 2 ounces of the chocolate with 1 teaspoon of coconut oil, either in the microwave or in a double boiler, until completely smooth.
3. Divide chocolate between the 4 cupcake liners, and put the plate in the freezer to harden while you prepare the peanut butter.
4. Mix peanut butter with powdered erythritol and a pinch of salt, to taste. This should create a thick, almost dough-like texture.
5. Make sure chocolate has solidified. Take plate out of freezer and divide peanut butter mixture between the 4 cups, keeping a small amount of space between the edge of the peanut butter and the edge of the liner. Return to freezer.
6. Melt the remaining 3 ounces of chocolate with 1 teaspoon coconut oil. Divide chocolate between the 4 cups, making sure the chocolate completely covers the peanut butter.
7. Return cups to the freezer to solidify for about 20 minutes before enjoying.
8. Cups can be stored at room temperature for a softer texture, or in the refrigerator for a firmer texture. Enjoy!

Dairy-free option: Use dairy-free chocolate.

Nut-free option: Use sunflower-seed butter instead of peanut butter.

Espresso Frosting, page 165

Frostings, Icings & Fillings

Chocolate Protein Frosting

Serves: 12

62 Calories / 5 g Fat / 1.5 g Net Carbs / 3 g Protein / 0.7 g Fiber / 1 g Sugar

INGREDIENTS:

5 tablespoons butter, room temperature (70 g)
1½ scoops chocolate whey protein powder (42 g)
¼ cup cocoa powder (20 g)
1 cup powdered erythritol* (192 g)
1 tablespoon pure maple syrup (15 ml)
¼ cup warm water (60 ml)

Tip! Regular powdered sugar or other powdered sweeteners may also be used.

Ⓖ Gluten-free
Ⓝ Nut-free
Ⓔ Egg-free
Ⓖ Grain-free

INSTRUCTIONS:

1. Combine all ingredients in a bowl and stir until very smooth.
2. Frost cake and enjoy!
3. Store in the refrigerator.

See this frosting on the Triple-Layer Chocolate Cake on page 2.

Plant-based/Dairy-free option: Use dairy-free butter.

Keto option: Use sugar-free syrup.

Espresso Frosting

Serves 12

123 calories / 13 g Fat / 0.8 g Net Carbs / 0.7 g Protein / 0 g Fiber / 1 g Sugar

INGREDIENTS:

5 tablespoons butter (70 g)
½ cup mascarpone (120 g)
2 tablespoons milk (30 ml)
1½ teaspoons instant espresso
1 cup powdered erythritol (192 g)

Tip! Other powdered sugar-free sweeteners, regular powdered sugar, or a combination may also be used.

G Gluten-free
N Nut-free
K Keto
S Sugar-free
E Egg-free
G Grain-free

INSTRUCTIONS:

1. Allow butter and mascarpone to come to room temperature.
2. Warm milk slightly and dissolve espresso powder in the milk.
3. Add the milk + espresso mixture to a bowl, then add remaining ingredients.
4. Beat with the whisk attachment of an electric mixer, starting at low speed and increasing speed until frosting is smooth and whipped.
5. Frost and enjoy!
6. Store in the refrigerator.

Tips: Mascarpone can be replaced with cream cheese, if necessary, but the cream cheese will add a slightly tangy flavor. Regular instant coffee can also be used if instant espresso is unavailable.

See this frosting on the Pumpkin Spice Latte Cupcakes on page 4.

Plant-based/Dairy-free option: Use dairy-free milk, dairy-free butter, and dairy-free cream cheese instead of mascarpone.

Cookie Dough Frosting

Serves 4

54 calories / 1.8 g Fat / 4.3 g Net Carbs / 4 g Protein / 1.5 g Fiber / 3.5 g Sugar

INGREDIENTS:

¼ scoop vanilla protein powder (7 g)
2 teaspoons unsweetened almond milk
¼ cup fat-free plain Greek yogurt (60 g)
2 tablespoons coconut flour (14 g)
1 teaspoon coconut sugar
⅛ teaspoon salt
2 teaspoons powdered erythritol or baking stevia
1 tablespoon chocolate chips (15 g)
¼ teaspoon vanilla

G Gluten-free
E Egg-free
G Grain-free

INSTRUCTIONS:

1. Dissolve protein powder in almond milk. Add Greek yogurt, and stir.
2. Add remaining ingredients and stir until combined.
3. Store in the refrigerator.

See this frosting on the Mini Double-Layer Brownie Cake on page 28.

Plant-based/Dairy-free: Use dairy-free and/or plant-based protein powder, and use dairy-free cream cheese or yogurt instead of the Greek yogurt.

Nut-free option: Use nut-free milk or water instead of almond milk.

Sugar-free option: Use sugar-free sweetener instead of coconut sugar, and use sugar-free chocolate chips.

Chocolate Brownie Frosting

Serves 4

30 calories / 0.5 g Fat / 5.5 g Net Carbs / 1 g Protein / 2 g Fiber / 3 g Sugar

INGREDIENTS:

¼ cup cocoa powder (20 g)
2 tablespoons powdered erythritol or baking stevia
2 teaspoons tapioca starch
1 tablespoon pure maple syrup (15 ml)
2 tablespoons unsweetened almond milk (30 ml)

G Gluten-free
P Plant-based
D Dairy-free
E Egg-free
G Grain-free

INSTRUCTIONS:

1. Combine cocoa, stevia, and starch in a small bowl. Add maple syrup.
2. Add almond milk slowly until desired consistency is reached.
3. Frost and enjoy!
4. Store in the refrigerator.

See this recipe on the Mini Double-Layer Brownie Cake on page 28.

Nut-free option: Use nut-free milk instead of almond milk.

Sugar-free option: Use sugar-free syrup instead of maple syrup.

Dark Chocolate Buttercream Frosting

Serves 16

24 calories / 1 g Fat / 2 g Net Carbs / 2 g Protein / 0 g Fiber / 1 g Sugar

INGREDIENTS:

⅔ scoop chocolate protein powder (18 g)

¼ cup Dutch-process cocoa powder (20 g)

3 tablespoons powdered erythritol or baking stevia

¼ cup tablespoons unsweetened almond milk (60 ml)

2 teaspoons pure maple syrup

6 tablespoons reduced-fat cream cheese (90 g)

G Gluten-free

E Egg-free

G Grain-free

INSTRUCTIONS:

1. Combine protein powder, cocoa powder, and powdered sweetener in a small bowl.
2. Add almond milk and maple syrup, and stir until dry ingredients have dissolved.
3. Add cream cheese and stir until very smooth.
4. Frost and enjoy!
5. Store in the refrigerator.

Find the recipe for these 5-Ingredient Brownies (pictured) on page 56.

Plant-based/Dairy-free: Use dairy-free and/or plant-based protein powder, and dairy-free cream cheese.

Nut-free option: Use nut-free milk instead of almond milk.

Sugar-free option: Use sugar-free syrup instead of maple syrup.

Creamy Mint Frosting

Serves: 16

8 calories / 0 g Fat / 1 g Net Carbs / 1 g Protein / 0 g Fiber / 0 g Sugar

INGREDIENTS:

¾ cup nonfat plain Greek yogurt (170 g)

1 tablespoon coconut flour (7 g)

¼ teaspoon peppermint extract

3 tablespoons powdered erythritol or baking stevia, or as needed to taste

⅛–¼ teaspoon spirulina (optional, for color)

G Gluten-free
N Nut-free
S Sugar-free
E Egg-free
G Grain-free

INSTRUCTIONS:

1. Combine all ingredients in a small bowl and stir until combined.
2. Spread evenly over cooled brownies.
3. Store in the refrigerator.

See this frosting on the Creamy Mint Chocolate Brownies on page 68.

Plant-based/Dairy-free: Use dairy-free yogurt or cream cheese, or a combination of the two, instead of Greek yogurt.

Keto option: Use full-fat Greek yogurt.

Salted Caramel Buttercream Frosting

Serves: 12

21 calories / 1 g Fat / 1 g Net Carbs / 1 g Protein / 0 g Fiber / 1 g Sugar

INGREDIENTS:

⅓ scoop vanilla whey protein powder (9 g)
1 teaspoon coconut sugar (4 g)
2–3 teaspoons unsweetened almond milk
   (10–15 ml)
6 tablespoons reduced-fat cream cheese (90 g)
Pinch of salt, to taste

G Gluten-free
E Egg-free
G Grain-free

INSTRUCTIONS:

1. Dissolve protein powder and coconut sugar in almond milk.
2. Add cream cheese and mix until smooth.
3. Add salt to taste.
4. Frost and enjoy!
5. Store in the refrigerator.

See this frosting on the White Chocolate Blondies on page 99.

Plant-based/Dairy-free: Use dairy-free and/or plant-based protein powder, and use dairy-free cream cheese.

Nut-free option: Use nut-free milk or water instead of almond milk.

Sugar-free option: Use sugar-free sweetener instead of coconut sugar, although this will remove the caramel flavor, so flavor extract or sugar-free caramel syrup may be used.

Low-Calorie Peanut Butter Drizzle

Serves 2

38 calories / 2 g Fat / 2 g Net Carbs / 3 g Protein / 1 g Fiber / 1 g Sugar

INGREDIENTS:

2 tablespoons powdered peanut butter (12 g)
1 tablespoon water (15 ml)
1 teaspoon peanut butter
Pinch of salt and stevia, to taste

G Gluten-free
P Plant-based
S Sugar-free
E Egg-free
G Grain-free

INSTRUCTIONS:

1. Combine all ingredients and stir until smooth. Use as a lower-calorie alternative to regular peanut butter!
2. Store in the refrigerator.

Vanilla Cream Frosting and Filling

Serves 8

42 calories / 0 g Fat / 3 g Net Carbs / 6 g Protein / 0.5 g Fiber / 3g Sugar

INGREDIENTS:

2 cups nonfat plain Greek yogurt (450 g)

⅓ cup powdered erythritol or baking stevia

2 tablespoons coconut flour (14 g)

2 teaspoons pure maple syrup

Ⓖ Gluten-free

Ⓝ Nut-free

Ⓔ Egg-free

Ⓖ Grain-free

INSTRUCTIONS:

1. Combine all ingredients in a bowl, and mix until well combined.

2. Add frosting to an icing bag to pipe, or use it as a filling.

3. Store in the refrigerator.

Sugar-free option: Use sugar-free syrup instead of maple syrup, or omit and use extra powdered sweetener.

Keto option: Use full-fat Greek yogurt and sugar-free syrup.

Edible Cookie Dough Filling I

Serves 8

55 calories / 2 g Fat / 4 g Net Carbs / 4 g Protein / 2 g Fiber / 4 g Sugar

INGREDIENTS:

½ scoop vanilla whey protein powder (14 g)

1⅓ tablespoons unsweetened almond milk (20 ml)

½ cup nonfat plain Greek yogurt (120 g)

2 teaspoon coconut palm sugar

2 tablespoons powdered erythritol or baking stevia

¼ cup coconut flour (28 g)

¼ teaspoon salt

½ teaspoon vanilla extract

2 tablespoons chocolate chips (30 g)

G Gluten-free

E Egg-free

INSTRUCTIONS:

1. Dissolve protein powder in almond milk. Add Greek yogurt, and stir.
2. Add remaining ingredients and stir until combined.
3. Store in the refrigerator.

See this filling in the brownie cups on page 71.

Plant-based/Dairy-free: Use dairy-free and/or plant-based protein powder, and use dairy-free cream cheese or yogurt instead of the Greek yogurt.

Nut-free option: Use nut-free milk instead of almond milk.

Sugar-free option: Use sugar-free sweetener instead of coconut sugar, and use sugar-free chocolate chips.

Edible Cookie Dough Filling II

Serves 12

102 calories / 4 g Fat / 14 g Net Carbs / 2 g Protein / 3 g Fiber / 10 g Sugar

INGREDIENTS:

½ cup coconut flour (56 g)
½ cup gluten-free all-purpose flour (74 g)
2 teaspoons ground flaxseed
¼ teaspoon salt
¼ cup maple syrup (60 ml)
¾ cup almond milk (180 ml)
½ cup chocolate chips (120 g)

(G) Gluten-free
(P) Plant-based
(D) Dairy-free
(E) Egg-free

INSTRUCTIONS:

1. Combine all dry ingredients (except chocolate chips).
2. Add wet ingredients and stir until a thick dough forms. Fold in chocolate chips.
3. Form into 12 balls.
4. Enjoy as is, or use as filling for cupcakes on page 36.

Nut-free option: Use nut-free milk instead of almond milk.

Paleo option: Use almond flour instead of all-purpose gluten-free flour.

Sugar-free option: Use sugar-free syrup instead of maple syrup, and use sugar-free chocolate chips.

Chocolate Peanut Butter Frosting

Serves 12

14 calories / 0.5g Fat / 1 g Net Carbs / 2 g Protein / 1 g Fiber / 0 g Sugar

INGREDIENTS:

½ scoop chocolate whey protein powder (14 g)
¼ cup powdered peanut butter (24 g)
3 tablespoons powdered erythritol or baking stevia
3 tablespoons cocoa powder (15 g)
3–4 tablespoons unsweetened almond milk, as
   needed (45–60 ml)

G Gluten-free
S Sugar-free
E Egg-free
G Grain-free

INSTRUCTIONS:

1. Combine all dry ingredients in a small bowl. Slowly add almond milk until desired consistency is reached.
2. Frost and enjoy!
3. Store in the refrigerator.

See this frosting on Peanut Butter Swirl Fudge Brownies on page 74.

> **Plant-based/Dairy-free:** Use dairy-free and/or plant-based protein powder.

Peanut Butter Frosting

Serves 1

76 calories / 2 g Fat / 7 g Net Carbs / 8 g Protein / 2 g Fiber / 5 g Sugar

INGREDIENTS:

3 tablespoons powdered peanut butter (18 g)
½ tablespoons unsweetened almond milk (23 ml)
1 tablespoon nonfat plain Greek yogurt (15 g)
2 teaspoons powdered erythritol or baking stevia

G Gluten-free
S Sugar-free
E Egg-free
G Grain-free

INSTRUCTIONS:

1. Combine powdered peanut butter with just enough almond milk to form a thick paste.
2. Add Greek yogurt.
3. Sweeten to taste with stevia.
4. Frost 1-Minute Chocolate Peanut Butter Cake on page 29 immediately before enjoying, or store in the refrigerator.

Plant-based/Dairy-free: Use dairy-free cream cheese instead of Greek yogurt.

Chocolate Buttercream Frosting

Serves 16

43 calories / 2.5 g Fat / 2 g Net Carbs / 2 g Protein / 0.5 g Fiber / 1.5 g Sugar

INGREDIENTS:

½ scoop chocolate whey protein powder (10 ml)

¼ cup cocoa powder (20 g)

¼ cup powdered erythritol (48 g)

2 teaspoons pure maple syrup (10 ml)

2 tablespoons unsweetened almond milk (15 ml)

½ cup reduced-fat cream cheese (120 g)

G Gluten-free

G Grain-free

E Egg-free

INSTRUCTIONS:

1. Combine protein powder, cocoa powder, and stevia in a small bowl.
2. Add almond milk and maple syrup and stir until dry ingredients have dissolved.
3. Add cream cheese and stir until very smooth.
4. Frost and enjoy!
5. Store in the refrigerator.

This frosting can be used as a nut-free frosting option for the Fudge Brownie Cookie Dough Cake on page 43.

Plant-based/Dairy-free: Use dairy-free and/or plant-based protein powder, and use dairy-free cream cheese.

Nut-free option: Use nut-free milk or water instead of almond milk.

Sugar-free option: Use sugar-free syrup instead of maple syrup, or omit and add extra powdered sweetener to taste.

Keto Icing Drizzle

Serves 9

0 calories / 0 g Fat / 0 g Net Carbs / 0 g Protein / 0 g Fiber / 0 g Sugar

INGREDIENTS:

5 tablespoons powdered erythritol (60 g)
2½ teaspoons water

G Gluten-free
P Plant-based
D Dairy-free
N Nut-free
K Keto
S Sugar-free
E Egg-free
G Grain-free

INSTRUCTIONS:

1. Prepare immediately before using.
2. Combine powdered erythritol and water and stir until smooth. If too thick, add a tiny bit more water. If too thin, add a tiny bit more erythritol.
3. Drizzle slowly over dessert in desired pattern, and enjoy!

See this drizzle on Keto Chocolate Chip Pound Cake on page 12.

3-Ingredient Chocolate Fudge Frosting

Serves 2

52 calories / 1.5 g Fat / 9.5 g Net Carbs / 2.5 g Protein / 5 g Fiber / 6.5 g Sugar

INGREDIENTS:

⅓ cup cocoa powder (27 g)
2 tablespoons powdered erythritol or baking stevia
1 tablespoon pure maple syrup (15 ml)
3 tablespoons water (45 ml)

(G) Gluten-free
(P) Plant-based
(N) Nut-free
(E) Egg-free
(G) Grain-free

INSTRUCTIONS:

1. In a small bowl, mix together cocoa powder and powdered sweetener.
2. Add maple syrup.
3. Slowly add water a little bit at a time until you reach the desired consistency.
4. Add extra sweetener to taste, if needed. Frost and enjoy!

This frosting can be used as a nut-free frosting option for the Fudge Brownie Cookie Dough Cake on page 43.

Sugar-free option: Use sugar-free syrup instead of maple syrup.

Keto Chocolate Fudge Frosting

Serves 12

77 calories / 8 g Fat / 0.5 g Net Carbs / 1 g Protein / 1.5 g Fiber / 0g Sugar

INGREDIENTS:

½ cup butter, softened (112 g)

1½ cups powdered erythritol (288 g)

½ cup cocoa powder (40 g)

2–3 teaspoons unsweetened almond milk (10 ml)

G Gluten-free

K Keto

S Sugar-free

E Egg-free

G Grain-free

INSTRUCTIONS:

1. Allow butter to come to room temperature.
2. Add softened butter, erythritol, and cocoa powder to a bowl, and stir until smooth.
3. Add milk 1 teaspoon at a time until desired texture is achieved.
4. Frost and enjoy!
5. Store in the refrigerator.

Tip! Use Dutch-process cocoa for dark chocolate frosting.

See this frosting on the Keto Vanilla Sheet Cake, page 11.

Plant-based/Dairy-free: Use dairy-free butter.

Nut-free: Use nut-free milk instead of almond milk.

Vanilla Whipped Cream

Serves 16

50 calories / 5 g Fat / 1 g Net Carbs / 0 g Protein / 0 g Fiber / 0 g Sugar

INGREDIENTS:

1 cup heavy cream (240 ml)

2 tablespoons powdered erythritol (24 g)

½ teaspoon vanilla extract or ¼ teaspoon vanilla
  bean powder

Ⓖ Gluten-free
Ⓝ Nut-free
Ⓚ Keto
Ⓢ Sugar-free
Ⓔ Egg-free
Ⓖ Grain-free

INSTRUCTIONS:

1. Beat heavy cream with electric mixer for about
   1 to 2 minutes until stiff peaks form.
2. Add erythritol and vanilla, and beat until
   combined.
3. Adjust sweetener to taste if needed.
4. Use as a topping for anything your heart
   desires!
5. Store in the refrigerator.

Sugar Cookie Buttercream Icing

Serves: 15

27 Calories / 3 g Fat / 0 g Net Carbs / 0 g Protein / 0 g Fiber / 0 g Sugar

INGREDIENTS:
¼ cup unsalted butter, room temperature (56 g)
1 cup powdered erythritol (192 g)
1 tablespoon water (15 ml)

Tip! Regular powdered sugar may be used if you do not need the icing to be keto.

G Gluten-free
N Nut-free
K Keto
S Sugar-free
E Egg-free
G Grain-free

INSTRUCTIONS:
1. Mix softened butter, powdered sweetener, and water in a bowl until very smooth.
2. Frost sugar cookies, and enjoy!
3. Store in the refrigerator.

Dairy-free option: Use dairy-free butter.

Keto Cream Cheese Frosting

Serves 12

50 calories / 5 g Fat / 0 g Net Carbs / 0.5 g Protein / 0 g Fiber / 0.3 g Sugar

INGREDIENTS:

½ cup cream cheese, softened (112 g)
2 tablespoons butter, softened (28 g)
1 cup powdered erythritol (192 g)
¼ teaspoon vanilla extract

(G) Gluten-free
(N) Nut-free
(K) Keto
(S) Sugar-free
(E) Egg-free
(G) Grain-free

INSTRUCTIONS:

1. Allow butter and cream cheese to come to room temperature.
2. Combine softened butter and cream cheese together in a bowl.
3. Add erythritol and vanilla and mix until smooth.
4. Frost and enjoy!
5. Store in the refrigerator.

See this frosting on the Keto Carrot Cake on page 14 or the Keto Pumpkin Spice Cupcakes on page 16.

Plant-based/Dairy-free: Use dairy-free butter and cream cheese.

Cream Cheese Frosting I

Serves: 2

73 calories / 4.5 g Fat / 2 g Net Carbs / 6 g Protein / 0 g Fiber / 2 g Sugar

INGREDIENTS:

¼ scoop vanilla whey protein powder (7 g)

1–2 teaspoons unsweetened almond milk (5–10 ml)

3 tablespoons reduced-fat cream cheese (45 g)

2 tablespoons nonfat plain Greek yogurt (30 g)

2–3 tablespoons powdered erythritol or baking stevia, to taste

G Gluten-free

S Sugar-free

E Egg-free

G Grain-free

INSTRUCTIONS:

1. Dissolve protein powder in almond milk.
2. Add cream cheese and Greek yogurt and mix until very smooth. Sweeten to taste.
3. Frost and enjoy!
4. Store in the refrigerator.

See this frosting on the Red Velvet Cake for Two on page 22.

Plant-based/Dairy-free: Use dairy-free cream cheese instead of the regular cream cheese and Greek yogurt.

Keto option: Use 5 tablespoons full-fat cream cheese instead of the reduced-fat cream cheese and Greek yogurt.

Nut-free option: Use nut-free milk instead of almond milk.

Cream Cheese Frosting II

Serves 4

65 calories / 0.5 g Fat / 4 g Net Carbs / 9 g Protein / 1 g Fiber / 3 g Sugar

INGREDIENTS:

¼ scoop vanilla protein powder (7 g)

2 teaspoons unsweetened almond milk, or as needed (10 ml)

1 cup nonfat plain Greek yogurt (227 g)

3 tablespoons fat-free cream cheese (42 g)

¼ cup powdered erythritol or baking stevia, to taste

2 tablespoons coconut flour, as needed to thicken (14 g)

G Gluten-free
S Sugar-free
E Egg-free
G Grain-free

INSTRUCTIONS:

1. Dissolve protein powder in almond milk.
2. Add Greek yogurt, cream cheese, and sweetener. Add coconut flour if needed until you achieve desired texture.
3. Frost and enjoy!
4. Store in the refrigerator.

See this frosting on the Mini Double-Layer Carrot Cake on page 30.

Keto option: Use full-fat cream cheese instead of Greek yogurt, and use butter instead of the fat-free cream cheese Omit coconut flour.

Nut-free option: Use nut-free milk instead of almond milk.

Cream Cheese Frosting III

Serves 4

93 calories / 3 g Fat / 4 g Net Carbs / 9 g Protein / 2 g Fiber / 4 g Sugar

INGREDIENTS:

⅓ scoop vanilla whey protein powder (9 g)

2 teaspoons unsweetened almond milk, as needed (10 ml)

1 cup nonfat plain Greek yogurt (227 g)

¼ cup reduced-fat cream cheese (60 g)

2 tablespoons coconut flour (14 g)

1 teaspoon pure maple syrup

3 tablespoons stevia, or to taste

G Gluten-free

E Egg-free

G Grain-free

INSTRUCTIONS:

1. Dissolve protein powder in almond milk.
2. Add yogurt and cream cheese, and stir until combined.
3. Add coconut flour until desired thickness is achieved, then add sweeteners to taste.
4. Frost and enjoy!

See this frosting on the Double-Layer Funfetti Brownie on page 88.

Keto option: Use full-fat cream cheese instead of Greek yogurt, and use butter instead of the reduced-fat cream cheese. Use sugar-free syrup instead of maple syrup.

Sugar-free option: Use sugar-free syrup instead of maple syrup.

Nut-free option: Use nut-free milk instead of almond milk.

Cream Cheese Frosting IV

Serves: 12

16 calories / 1 g Fat / 0.8 g Net Carbs / 1 g Protein / 0.2 g Fiber / 0.8 g Sugar

INGREDIENTS:

½ cup nonfat plain Greek yogurt (113 g)
¼ cup reduced-fat cream cheese (60 g)
1 tablespoon coconut flour (7 g)
1 teaspoon pure maple syrup
2–3 tablespoons powdered erythritol or baking
    stevia, or to taste

G Gluten-free
N Nut-free
E Egg-free
G Grain-free

INSTRUCTIONS:

1. Combine Greek yogurt, cream cheese, and maple syrup in a small bowl.
2. Add coconut flour until you achieve desired texture.
3. Sweeten with stevia to taste.
4. Frost and enjoy!

See this frosting on Sugar Cookie Blondies on page 97.

Keto option: Use full-fat cream cheese instead of Greek yogurt, and use butter instead of the reduced-fat cream cheese. Use sugar-free syrup instead of maple syrup.

Sugar-free option: Use sugar-free syrup instead of maple syrup.

Acknowledgments

To Mom and Dad, thank you for showing me what it takes to succeed as an entrepreneur, and for wholeheartedly supporting my atypical postcollege career trajectory. This cookbook would not have been possible without you.

Thank you to my younger brothers, William and Dylan, for being honest taste testers (picky eaters tend to be the best testers), as well as my co-bakers for many holiday and birthday occasions.

Thank you to my Grandmother Ellen, for passing down your baking and cooking genes. I still cannot bake banana bread as good as yours, but I will keep trying.

To my Grandfather Al, thank you for instilling a sense of imagination and determination in me that has led me to successfully achieve my dreams. I know you would be so proud of this book.

Thank you to all of the other family members who helped raise me, including my Grandmother Louise, my Grandfather Charlie, and all of my aunts, uncles, and cousins.

Juliana, my best friend who happens to be my second cousin, thank you for being my constant source of support. We text each other almost every hour of every day, so you have been there for the entirety of this cookbook being developed, talking me through every struggle and triumph that came up along the way.

Olivia, thank you for encouraging me to never be ashamed of self-promotion. I remember seeing you the day before I launched my first e-book, feeling unsure of myself, and you were the person who convinced me that it was a great idea.

To Michaella, for always sending me breaking news articles on the latest Instagram features, security breaches, and baking-product recalls, as well as your help finishing an e-book design project gone wrong. Thank you for all the time and effort you put into my project, for no reason other than to help and support me.

Samantha, thank you for being my #1 hype woman and telling everyone you meet about what I do. The fact that you still call me "Sarah Lynn Fitness" (my first Instagram username) no matter how much effort I put into rebranding myself always makes me laugh.

To Tim, for being both my taste tester and my person to unwind with after long days of recipe testing and photoshoots. Thank you for your brilliant business advice and believing in my ability to take my career further than I could ever imagine possible. Most importantly, thank you for always polishing everything off, so no baked goods ever go to waste.

To all of my other friends, thank you for supporting my unique career path and for always being there to encourage me.

To my Skyhorse Publishing team, thank you for all of your hard work on this book. Special thanks to my editor, Nicole Frail, for being understanding and considerate every step of the way, and always taking my opinions into account when making decisions about the book.

Thank you to all of my readers and social media followers, especially those who have purchased my e-books. Without your support, this book would not exist, and I will never be able to thank you enough for believing in me.

About the Author

Sarah has always had a passion for baking, as well as a huge sweet tooth. Growing up, she looked forward to birthdays and holidays because it meant an opportunity to decorate cookies, build gingerbread houses, or bake elaborate tri-ple-layer birthday cakes. But unfortunately, due to their unhealthy nature, these treats were mainly reserved for special occasions.

Sarah attended the University of Richmond in Virginia, where she earned a bachelor's degree in Studio Art and Business Administration. During her time at Richmond, she developed a passion for health and fitness, leading her to launch her first Instagram account, @sarahlynnfitness (later rebranded as @sarahsfitfood). This early social media account gave her the platform to share healthy eating and fitness tips, as well as connect with others who had similar interests.

With a desire to combine her two passions—baking and health—Sarah began exploring alternative baking ingredients that would provide more health benefits than the traditionally used refined flour, sugar, and oils. Discovering that she needed to commit to a gluten-free diet only further inspired her to experiment with her own baking recipes. By using healthy ingredients in new and creative ways, she was able to create dessert recipes that are gluten-free, free of refined sugar, and allergen-friendly, as well as being higher in protein and lower in calories, carbs, and total sugar.

The results were shocking. Everyone Sarah shared her healthy desserts with could not believe that they were actually healthy. She realized that, with a bit of creativity and experimentation, she had the ability to create desserts that look and taste extremely decadent but are suitable to be enjoyed on a regular basis—for dessert, snacks, or even for breakfast.

Sarah began sharing delicious photos and videos along with the recipes on her Instagram account, @sarahsfitfood, and they were a huge hit. Soon after, she launched a second Instagram account, @baketobefit, to showcase her readers' re-creations of the recipes.

Needless to say, many significant accomplishments have occurred since Sarah graduated from college in May 2015. Sarah has built a social media empire, supporting the release of five incredibly popular eCookbooks, as well as a website that has become a go-to baking resource for hundreds of thousands of people worldwide. She has incorporated her company Bake to Be Fit, and the e-books and this cookbook are only the beginning of what she intends to develop for the company in the future. Sarah has been featured on *Business Insider*, *Buzzfeed*, *The LADbible*, *UNILAD*, *VT*, *Fortafy*, *Boston Voyager Magazine*, and *Spoon University*, among many other media outlets. Her viral videos have received well over 100 million cumulative views.

When she's not dreaming up new recipes, Sarah enjoys traveling, live music, indoor cycling, running, visiting new gluten-free bakeries, and exploring everything her home city of Boston has to offer.

Index

Conversion Charts

METRIC AND IMPERIAL CONVERSIONS

(These conversions are rounded for convenience)

Ingredient	Cups/Tablespoons/Teaspoons	Ounces	Grams/Milliliters
Butter	1 cup/ 16 tablespoons/ 2 sticks	8 ounces	230 grams
Cream cheese	1 tablespoon	0.5 ounce	14.5 grams
Cornstarch	1 tablespoon	0.3 ounce	8 grams
Flour, all-purpose (gluten-free)	1 cup	5.2 ounces	148 grams
Fruit, dried	1 cup	4 ounces	120 grams
Fruits or veggies, chopped	1 cup	5 to 7 ounces	145 to 200 grams
Fruits or veggies, pureed	1 cup	8.5 ounces	245 grams
Honey, maple syrup, or corn syrup	1 tablespoon	0.75 ounce	20 grams
Liquids: cream, milk, water, or juice	1 cup	8 fluid ounces	240 milliliters
Oats	1 cup	5.5 ounces	150 grams
Salt	1 teaspoon	0.2 ounce	6 grams
Spices: cinnamon, cloves, ginger, or nutmeg (ground)	1 teaspoon	0.2 ounce	5 milliliters
Sugar, brown, firmly packed	1 cup	7 ounces	200 grams
Sugar, white	1 cup/1 tablespoon	7 ounces/0.5 ounce	200 grams/12.5 grams
Vanilla extract	1 teaspoon	0.2 ounce	4 grams

OVEN TEMPERATURES

Fahrenheit	Celsius	Gas Mark
225°	110°	¼
250°	120°	½
275°	140°	1
300°	150°	2
325°	160°	3
350°	180°	4
375°	190°	5
400°	200°	6
425°	220°	7
450°	230°	8